At Issue

| The Children
of Undocumented
Immigrants

Other Books in the At Issue Series:

At Issue

The Children
of Undocumented
Immigrants

David Haugen and Susan Musser, Book Editors

GREENHAVEN PRESS
A part of Gale, Cengage Learning

GALE
CENGAGE Learning·

Detroit • New York • San Francisco • New Haven, Conn • Waterville, Maine • London

Elizabeth Des Chenes, *Director, Publishing Solutions*

For more information, contact:
Greenhaven Press
27500 Drake Rd.
Farmington Hills, MI 48331-3535
Or you can visit our Internet site at gale.cengage.com

For product information and technology assistance, contact us at

Gale Customer Support, 1-800-877-4253
For permission to use material from this text or product, submit all requests online at www.cengage.com/permissions

Further permissions questions can be e-mailed to permissionrequest@cengage.com

Articles in Greenhaven Press anthologies are often edited for length to meet page requirements. In addition, original titles of these works are changed to clearly present the main thesis and to explicitly indicate the author's opinion. Every effort is made to ensure that Greenhaven Press accurately reflects the original intent of the authors. Every effort has been made to trace the owners of copyrighted material.

Cover image © Images.com/Corbis.

LIBRARY OF CONGRESS CATALOGING-IN-PUBLICATION DATA

The children of undocumented immigrants / David Haugen and Susan Musser, book editors.
  pages cm. -- (At issue)
  Includes bibliographical references and index.
  ISBN 978-0-7377-6159-7 (hbk.) -- ISBN 978-0-7377-6160-3 (pbk.)
  1. Children of immigrants--United States. 2. Children of immigrants--Education--United States. 3. Children of immigrants--Legal status, laws, etc.--United States. 4. Emigration and immigration law--United States. 5. Aliens--Family relationships--United States. I. Haugen, David M., 1969- editor. II. Musser, Susan, editor.
  HQ792.U5C4345 2013
  305.23'0973--dc23
                                                            2012051660

Printed in the United States of America
1 2 3 4 5 6 7 17 16 15 14 13

Contents

Introduction

In its most recent analysis, the Pew Hispanic Center, part of a nonpartisan research institution, estimated that the number of US-born children of undocumented immigrants residing in the United States was roughly four million in 2008. That number is up from around 2.7 million in 2003, according to the center, because of increased immigration and because of the relatively youthful age of those who come to work and start families in America. In fact, according to the Pew study, nearly half of undocumented households (47 percent) in 2008 consist of a married or unmarried couple with children; this is greater than the share of households of US-born residents with children (21 percent) and legal immigrants with children (35 percent). Seventy-six percent of these children come from families with roots in Hispanic parts of the world (chiefly Mexico, but also South and Central America), while Asia is the next highest contributing region with a mere 11 percent.

The Pew Hispanic Center also maintains that 73 percent of children of unauthorized immigrants are US citizens because they were born in the United States. The government affords them this status and its protections because Congress and the US Supreme Court have held that the Citizenship Clause of the Fourteenth Amendment affirms that "[a]ll persons born or naturalized in the United States, and subject to the jurisdiction thereof, are citizens of the United States." Therefore, while immigration services may act to deport undocumented immigrant parents, it has no authority to forcibly evict their children based on the children's familial relation. This legal tradition, however, has not prevented some commentators and legislators from insisting that the Fourteenth Amendment has been misinterpreted, alleging that the drafters of the Citizenship Clause were making amends for slavery and not intending to confer such rights to children of immigrants who were not legal citizens themselves. Republican state senator of Arizona Russell Pearce argued this viewpoint when, on July 30, 2010, he was quoted by the *Wall Street Journal* as stating, "When it was ratified in 1868, the amendment had to do with African-Americans; it had nothing to do with aliens. . . . It's got to be fixed." According to Pearce and like-minded others, the amendment as written only confers citizenship on individuals "subject to the jurisdiction" of the United States and not on undocumented immigrants or their children. Pearce's comments stoked national debate over the issue and brought renewed attention to the growing population of children with undocumented parents.

The status of children who came to the United States as immigrants but who have spent most of their lives in the country are also at the forefront of this debate. Ragini Shah, a clinical professor of law at Boston's Suffolk University Law School, wrote a research paper published by the university in May 2009 in which she explained how many of the undocumented long-term resident children she works with feel confused about their citizenship status. "The young people . . . identify as American. Many do not realize that they are not US citizens because they only have memories of life in the United States," Shah asserts. "I raise the self-identification of these young people to relate their high degree of integration into the national community and their sense of belonging in the United States. The latter is an important part of their claims to US citizenship under a more inclusive citizenship framework. This is not to suggest that one's sense of belonging is itself sufficient to justify citizenship claims. However, when it is combined with indications that the state has started to integrate them as members of the community, we must reconsider their continued exclusion from formal citizenship." Shah indicates that the state has made such overtures to immigrants and their children over the past few decades, including the passage of the Immigration Reform and Control Act of 1986, which provided a path toward residency for aliens who registered between 1987 and 1988, as well as President Barack Obama's executive policy to halt the deportation of some young undocumented immigrants starting in 2012. In addition, the state provides education benefits and limited welfare for undocumented children, showing another degree of inclusivity.

Perhaps the most enduring barometer of the national attitude toward citizenship for undocumented children is the ongoing introduction of the Development, Relief, and Education for Alien Minors (DREAM) Act to Congress. Since 2001, versions of the bill have been debated on the House and Senate floor. The act proposes to offer temporary residency to children who are in the United States illegally but who choose to complete either two years of military service or two years of higher education. Supporters and detractors have been active both in Congress and in the public sphere every time DREAM Act legislation arises. When the bill came up in 2010, the American Legion posted its opposition to passage. "Every parent wants the best opportunities for their child, yet the DREAM Act forces us to provide opportunities for the children of those who entered the country illegally at the same level of our own citizens," said Tim Tetz, legislative director of the American Legion, in a December 13, 2010, posting on the institution's website. "It is unfair the American taxpayers would be forced to subsidize the education of children of illegal aliens." Alternately, the progressive organization Change.org argued in their petition in support of the DREAM Act in 2011 that "if Congress fails to act this year, another entire class of outstanding, law-abiding high school students will graduate without being able to plan for the future, and some will be removed from their homes to countries they barely know."

In *At Issue: The Children of Undocumented Immigrants*, debates over the status of these young people bring to light the core ideals that structure the pro and con arguments regarding immigration policy and a related understanding of the principles that guide the nation. Some wish to foster a tighter rein on immigration to make sure that those who are in the country illegally—including children—do not gain privileges while flouting the country's laws. Others note that the path to legal immigration now has innumerable obstacles and invoke the historical fact that America has always been a nation of immigrants that welcomes those seeking opportunity. Caught in the middle of the debate are the four million US-born children of undocumented immigrants. For many observers, the plight of these children will not be satisfactorily addressed until the nation's immigration policy is reformed. As President Obama stated in a May 10, 2011, speech on the Texas border, "We need to come together around reform that reflects our values as a nation of laws and a nation of immigrants; reform that demands that everybody take responsibility."

1

Children of Illegal Immigrants Deserve Better Educational Options

Ron Haskins and Marta Tienda

Ron Haskins is a senior editor of The Future of Children, *a social service journal jointly published by the Brookings Institution and Princeton University. Marta Tienda is a professor of demographic studies and sociology at Princeton University.*

Immigrant children—particularly Latino children of undocumented aliens—often suffer both low educational opportunities and outcomes in the United States. Because the success of these young generations is a product of their education, the American government and education system should do more to help immigrant children. Specifically, the nation should provide preschool education to low-income immigrant children, improve language instruction for older children, and permit these kids to help themselves and the country by allowing them to enroll in higher education or join the military. Indeed, affording children of immigrants the opportunity to become citizens and benefit the United States would be a testament to the nation's belief in and commitment to the American dream.

Major federal immigration legislation in 1965 changed the criteria for gaining admission to the United States from a quota system that favored European immigrants to one that gave priority to family reunification. Although the immigrants from a single country cannot exceed 7 percent of total immigration in a year, unmarried children, spouses, and parents of U.S. citizens are exempted from the country caps. The 1965 reforms had two unintended consequences: the volume of immigrants surged, and newcomers' countries of origin shifted from Europe to Asia and Latin America.

Poor Educational Outcomes Among Latino Children

The result, as shown by Jeffrey Passel in the spring 2011 issue of *The Future of Children*, has been the greatest influx of immigrants to this country since the turn of the nineteenth century. The United States has legally admitted an average of about 1 million immigrants a year since 1990, and an average of about 500,000 each year have entered illegally or overstayed their visas. Mexicans are the largest single immigrant group, and many of them are unauthorized. According to the U.S. Census Bureau, 53 percent of immigrants are from Latin America, and about 30 percent are Mexican. Currently estimated at 31 million, Mexicans (both native born and foreign born) account for about 10 percent of the U.S. population. Passel also points out another important consequence of this flow of immigrants: Today about 23 percent of all U.S. children are immigrants or the children of immigrants.

For each step up the educational ladder—from school dropout, to high school graduate, to having attended college, to two-year and four-year college degrees, to professional or graduate degrees—median household income rises.

In part because the majority of immigrants from Asian nations enter under employment preferences that require market skills, Asian immigrants and their children have fared quite well in the United States. Among all ethnic and racial groups in the United States, including whites, those of Asian origin have the highest levels of education and income. By contrast, immigrants from Latin America have fared poorly both in education and in earnings. In 2010, for example, nearly half of Asians had at least a bachelor's degree, compared with less than 10 percent of Latinos. The median income of Asian households in 2009 was $65,180, compared with $38,000 for Latinos generally and $36,800 for Mexicans specifically.

In their 2009 book examining Latino educational achievement, Patricia Gándara and Frances Contreras labeled this problem "The Latino Education Crisis." The list of education-related outcomes on which Latinos, but especially Mexicans, trail other ethnic groups is striking. The list includes achievement test performance at age five and earlier; performance in reading and math at grades four, eight and twelve; high school grade point average; and rates of high school graduation, college attendance, and college degree completion.

> *Low educational achievement among Latinos is one of the most important problems that limits the futures of immigrant children.*

School performance, including completed education levels, is correlated with social mobility and economic well-being. For each step up the educational ladder—from school dropout, to high school graduate, to having attended college, to two-year and four-year college degrees, to professional or graduate degrees—median household income rises. Some of the income gaps among families with varying levels of education are huge. The annual household income difference between high school dropouts and those with a four-year degree at ages thirty to thirty-nine was about $59,900 ($26,500 compared with $86,400) in 2009.

A Casual Relationship

Correlation is not causation. In the case of the link between education and family income, however, there is every indication that the relationship is causal. A seminal volume by Claudia Goldin and Lawrence Katz not only lays out in great detail the correlation between education and income, but also argues persuasively that inequality is increasing in the United States because growth in the fraction of Americans who graduate from high school and in the fraction who graduate from college is increasing slowly or falling. Recent trends send a powerful message: Increases in education are the surest way to income mobility; failure to raise low levels of education guarantees income stagnation. So problematic is the low level of Latino education that Gándara and Contreras conclude that "if the high dropout rates and low educational achievement of Latino youth are not turned around, we will have created a permanent underclass without hope of integrating into the mainstream."

Low educational achievement among Latinos is one of the most important problems that limits the futures of immigrant children. Latin American immigrants arrive in the United States with a strong work ethic and strong family values. But by the second generation, their work rates decline, their wage progress appears to slow, and both their nonmarital birth rates and their divorce rates rise. These social and economic trends bode ill for immigrant parents, their children, and the nation. Finding ways to boost achievement and help more Latinos complete high school and attend and complete college or other postsecondary training should be high on the nation's policy agenda.

Policies Needed to Address the Problem

Three policy changes hold promise for boosting education among immigrant children and could, over a generation or two, increase both family income and family stability. Specifically, the nation should provide preschool education to all low-income immigrant children, improve language instruction for school-age children, and pass a revised version of the Development, Relief, and Education for Alien Minors (DREAM) Act that would allow undocumented adolescents brought as children to the United States by their parents to attend post-secondary institutions or join the military services and subsequently become citizens. Combined, these three policies would bolster the human capital of young immigrants—the fastest-growing segment of the U.S. population—and could produce a demographic dividend for our aging population in the form of a larger and higher-earning workforce that contributes more to the Social Security and Medicare trust funds. Other policy analysts have proposed to address low educational achievement among immigrants by making fundamental changes in immigration policy, such as reducing the number of immigrants admitted because of family relationships in favor of admitting immigrants with more education or skills. Such changes in immigration policy may be desirable but are beyond the scope of this brief.

Expanding Preschool Programs

Immigrant children face a serious educational challenge even before they enter the public schools. A disproportionate number of them have mothers with little education and limited English fluency, both of which are associated with poor school readiness among their children and with subsequent academic problems. Several national studies show that an achievement gap between immigrant children and native children (those born in the United States to U.S. parents) opens during the preschool years and does not close during the primary or middle school years. One intervention that demonstrably promotes early development and can help prevent the preschool gap from opening is high-quality preschool programs.

In the new spring 2011 volume of *The Future of Children*, Lynn Karoly and Gabriella Gonzalez examine research on early education programs for immigrant children and explain why expanded preschool programs should be part of a national strategy to prevent the achievement gap. First, they point out that many quality preschool programs now help children from poor families and immigrant families improve their language and math readiness for the public schools, with benefits continuing during the school years and beyond. A program for four-year-olds in Oklahoma, for example, substantially increased the school readiness of Latino children as measured by standardized tests. Second, the authors note that immigrant children are less likely to participate in out-of-home care than are nonimmigrant children. Only about 45 percent of immigrant three-year-olds and 65 percent of four-year-olds are in center-based facilities, and many of these facilities provide mediocre care that will not give the needed boost to the children's development.

> *Compelling evidence . . . shows that increasing the number of immigrant children in high-quality preschool programs will boost their school achievement.*

Third, although immigrant children's low rate of preschool enrollment is attributable not to their immigrant status per se but rather to family characteristics such as high poverty rates, low maternal education, and the daily presence at home of one parent in a two-parent family, extending preschool programs to more immigrant children makes sense because they are likely to be raised in low-income homes where parents speak limited English. Fourth, making preschool programs available to more immigrant children and directing outreach to their parents could help break down barriers to preschool enrollment, such as the reluctance of undocumented parents to have contact with public officials, the inability of low-income parents to pay for high-quality care, and the difficulties for parents with limited English skills of completing complex paperwork to enroll their children in preschool and apply for subsidies.

All students benefit academically when schools implement instructional programs proven successful with English language learners.

Compelling evidence, then, shows that increasing the number of immigrant children in high-quality preschool programs will boost their school achievement. But what of the increasing pressure on federal spending? One possible strategy would be to allow states that are willing to expand their prekindergarten programs for low-income children, including immigrant children, to take control of Head Start funding in their state. A high-quality national evaluation shows that the federal Head Start program is not adequately preparing preschoolers for the public schools. By contrast, many evaluations seem to show that state pre-K programs promote school readiness for four-year-olds more effectively than Head Start does. States, then, might be able to produce greater benefits for all poor children, including immigrant children, than does the current Head Start program. At the very least, Congress should give the Department of Health and Human Services the authority to experiment by allowing a few states, notably those with large immigrant populations, to control Head Start funding in exchange for admitting more low-income and immigrant children to high-quality programs and agreeing to have their programs rigorously evaluated.

Instituting Better Programs for English Language Learners

Another article in the spring 2011 volume of *The Future of Children*, by Margarita Calderón, Robert Slavin, and Malta

Sánchez, points out that during the 2007–08 school year 5.3 million students (10.6 percent of all students) were English language learners (ELLs). About 80 percent of these students were Spanish speaking. Although the Supreme Court in *Lau v. Nichols* (1974) ruled that schools are responsible for providing special assistance to non-English-speaking students, a national survey showed that in 2000, 41 percent of all U.S. teachers instructed English learners, but only 13 percent of teachers had received any specialized training in effective methods for teaching students who are not proficient in English. Given the universal finding from research that English learners fall behind other students in academic achievement, as well as the evidence that achievement gaps are relatively stable after third grade, it follows that helping English learners master English by second grade is an essential policy target to boost academic achievement of immigrant children.

The field of ELL instruction has long been divided between those who believe that English learners should have bilingual instruction and those who believe all instruction should be in English. But, say Calderón and her co-authors, a review of the relevant research shows that the conflict between the competing views obscures the real issue—namely, that the quality of the instruction is more important than whether it is bilingual or English immersion. And they find that effective programs feature frequent data collection on student learning, professional development that helps teachers learn to use curriculums and offers them coaching or other ways to practice classroom skills, and effective classroom and school management in which information about students is widely shared and all staff are held accountable for student learning. A small number of curriculums, including the Success for All whole-school reform model, have been shown by rigorous evaluations to improve both the English skills and the achievement of English learners. What is more, all students benefit academically when schools implement instructional programs proven successful with English language learners.

The [Barack] Obama administration has launched several initiatives that allocate funding to states and other entities to implement programs that have been shown by rigorous evaluation to produce good outcomes—the idea being that federal dollars should support programs based on solid evidence of effectiveness. The review by Calderón and her colleagues identifies several evidence-based programs that improve both English learning and academic performance; one, the Success for All program, is already being expanded using federal funds. If the evaluations from the expansion continue to be positive for immigrant children, Congress and the administration should continue to expand the program to other schools.

If immigrant families knew that their children could attend college and achieve citizenship, the children might work harder in school to prepare for college.

Pass the DREAM Act

In today's global economy most young people in the United States, native or immigrant, will need some postsecondary education to earn enough to support a family. Latinos, not surprisingly, are far less likely to enroll in any form of postsecondary education than are either natives or other immigrant groups. Policies that raise postsecondary enrollment and completion rates can help not only Latinos but all immigrants achieve financial stability while boosting the economy by providing a skilled workforce for American employers. To the extent that immigrants and children of immigrants can get a postsecondary education, they will help themselves, their families, and the American economy.

One way to increase immigrant postsecondary education would be to focus on undocumented immigrant youth who were brought to the United States as children by their parents. Under current law, these young adults are subject to deportation, cannot receive benefits designed to defray college costs for students from poor families, and cannot work. Yet many have excelled in high school and are well qualified for college. Moreover, if immigrant families knew that their children could attend college and achieve citizenship, the children might work harder in school to prepare for college and their parents too might put a greater emphasis on their schoolwork.

The DREAM Act, first introduced in Congress in 2001, would give certain undocumented students the opportunity both to attend college and to become citizens by following a two-step process. The first step gives undocumented youth a conditional legal status that allows them to work or attend school without fear of deportation. To qualify, youth must be enrolled in a two-year or four-year college or in trade school, have a high school diploma or General Educational Development credential, have been in the United States continuously for at least five years, have good moral character, and meet a few other requirements. Then, in the second step, youth would have up to six years to apply to upgrade their status to legal permanent resident (LPR), which in turn would allow them to apply for citizenship. To upgrade their status to LPR and eventually citizenship, immigrant youth would be required, among other things, to maintain good moral character and complete at least two years of college, trade school, or military service. During the second step, the youth would be eligible for federal student loans and some other benefits, but not Pell grants (the major source of federal grant funds for low-income college students) or welfare benefits. . . .

In 2010, the DREAM Act's most recent congressional run, it passed the House but was defeated in the Senate, when supporters could not muster the sixty votes needed to end a filibuster. The major arguments against the act are that it would reward illegal behavior (unauthorized entry to the United

States) by granting what opponents call "amnesty," allow "criminal aliens" to become citizens, cost taxpayers money by allowing some federal and state funds to be spent on undocumented immigrants and thereby deprive some citizens of educational benefits, and allow aliens granted LPR status the right to bring their relatives to the United States. Opponents also argue that by rewarding unauthorized entry, the act would encourage future illegal entry to the United States.

The [DREAM] act will help immigrant youth by boosting their education and will help the nation by allowing it to recoup the investments it has made in their K-12 education.

Although the opposing sides in the immigration debate appear to be mired in cement, it nonetheless seems worthwhile to consider in a reasoned and measured way the possibility that the DREAM Act would help immigrant children and, for that matter, the nation. Reliable information, some of it from social science research, bears on most points of contention. Take the cost of the bill. [The] CBO [Congressional Budget Office] says the bill would reduce the deficit by $1.4 billion over its first ten years and cost a few hundred million dollars a year thereafter. Proponents of the bill argue that the CBO estimate does not take into account the financial and nonfinancial effects of improving the education of the approximately 1.1 million youth expected to take advantage of the legislation. Opponents argue that the bill would result in a big influx of new immigrants, many of whom would consume federal and state resources, because youth who have reached age twenty-one and upgraded to LPR status could sponsor their immediate relatives for entry to the United States.

The concern that large numbers of family members would be sponsored for entry could be easily allayed by enforcing the sponsorship obligations already in place and raising the income threshold for sponsorship from 125 percent of poverty to 200 percent or higher. The charge that the bill would grant amnesty is correct. But the amnesty would go only to a select group of youth—those who have either served in the military or completed at least two years of postsecondary education—and would thus fulfill a key purpose of immigration policy, which has always been to admit people who could help build the nation. Moreover, being brought to the United States illegally by their parents as children hardly seems to qualify as an illegal act by the youth. In fact, the DREAM Act is in accord with an important principle of U.S. law, which is that children are not fully responsible for their actions.

Showing Faith in the American Way

Perhaps the two strongest arguments in favor of the DREAM Act are that giving people a chance based on academic achievement and good behavior is the American way and that the act will help immigrant youth by boosting their education and will help the nation by allowing it to recoup the investments it has made in their K-12 education. A careful study by Neeraj Kaushal of Columbia University found that allowing Mexican youth to pay in-state tuition for postsecondary education would increase their high school graduation rate by 14 percent, their college enrollment by 31 percent, and the number with a college degree by 33 percent—precisely the types of outcomes the nation needs to close education gaps between immigrant and native youth. If the incentive provided by offering young immigrants in-state tuition generates benefits of this magnitude, the joint impact of offering both in-state tuition (which would be encouraged by the DREAM Act) and the promise of a pathway to American citizenship should provide even greater motivation for undocumented immigrant youth to raise their academic achievement. Few policies are as likely to boost postsecondary education among immigrant youth as the DREAM Act.

Taken together, these three policies would increase the school readiness of immigrant children, increase the odds that young immigrant children speak English well enough not to fall behind in their subject matter achievement, and increase the rates of postsecondary education among immigrant youth. The short- and long-term effects on immigrant children, their families, and society would be positive; achieving these changes could guide future immigration reform in ways that would better align democratic principles and economic goals.

2

Children of Illegal Immigrants Deserve In-State College Tuition Rates

Mary Sanchez

Mary Sanchez is an op-ed columnist for the Kansas City Star *newspaper.*

While various Republican politicians and commentators are criticizing Texas Governor Rick Perry for supporting his state's decision to grant in-state tuition to those children of illegal immigrants who are seeking higher education, he must stand firm. Individual states and the nation as a whole should recognize that education is a path to legal status and an economic benefit to America. These immigrants have paid taxes and have earned the right to send their kids to school. If the federal government has stalled in addressing immigration issues, the states need to show their compassion and determination to do the right thing.

Texas Gov. Rick Perry missed his teachable moment. But he shouldn't fret. He'll get another shot at it.

Perry chose a defensive posture when fellow GOP [Republican party] presidential candidates attacked over Texas's college in-state tuition option for children whose parents hauled them to this country illegally.

At a recent debate [in September 2011], Perry let others distort the issue. He flubbed it, and his opponents smelled blood in the water.

He may not realize it yet, but Perry's stumble harms more than just his own quest for the GOP presidential nomination.

Taking the Right Stance on Immigrant Education

It's imperative that Perry, who holds sway with conservatives, gets this right. He's being coached now. A lot of voices, from the *Wall Street Journal*'s editorial page to [former Governor of Arkansas] Mike Huckabee, are offering Perry advice on how to better explain his state's rational immigration positions. I hope he's listening. Perry's informed, pragmatic approach to the education of immigrants is rare these days among Republicans.

People who support such punitive measures on children, including Alabama's governor, ought to spend a few days doing the work that isn't getting done around the state as the parents of those children . . . have been scared off.

States are enacting measures targeting those least responsible for the nation's immigration quandaries: children. And they are threatening the one thing beyond food, shelter and medical care that every child deserves: an education.

Consider Alabama. Among the provisions of a new law a federal judge declined to enter a preliminary injunction against: Public schools are to verify the legal status of students they enroll and that of their parents. They aren't to deny them entry into classrooms, but you can bet the effect will be chilling on enrollments. Which is exactly what the zealots are hoping for.

Maybe a little fresh air is what they need to clear their heads. People who support such punitive measures on children, including Alabama's governor, ought to spend a few days doing the work that isn't getting done around the state as the parents of those children, migrant laborers (some legal), have been scared off.

Alabama's agriculture commissioner has been telling horror stories of rotting crops in the fields. Unemployed native-born workers don't flock to fill vacancies in the fields.

Explaining these economic realities is exactly where Perry could have an impact.

Failed Policies and Humane Actions

The real problem is that we don't have a workable system to control who migrates, and for how long, especially for low-wage laborers.

As a *Wall Street Journal* editorial addressing Perry's gaffes pointedly argued: "Under our current system, it is nearly impossible for a typical Mexican to migrate to the U.S. legally within his lifetime. If the U.S. supplied enough work visas to meet demand, fewer migrants would have reason to enter illegally, and border resources could focus on genuine threats."

Bravo. This basic explanation of how the nation came to have 11 million undocumented immigrants, including their children, is suspiciously missing from public discussion.

Denying innocent children an education isn't going to fix the underlying problem, which is economic in nature.

Texas is dealing pragmatically and humanely with a consequence of failed federal immigration policy.

Texas, as a border state, knows that well. The 1982 U.S. Supreme Court decision mandating that undocumented children have a right to a public K-12 education, originated in Texas. And Texas was the first state to address what happens to those students after high school.

What Perry failed to explain is that, in order to qualify for in-state tuition at public colleges and universities, the students in question have to graduate from Texas high schools, to have lived in the state for at least three years and be seeking legal status.

There's no free handout. They and their families have been paying state taxes for years. Texas is dealing pragmatically and humanely with a consequence of failed federal immigration policy.

Are you listening [former Massachusetts governor and 2012 Republican nominee for president] Mitt Romney? If the GOP nominates and the nation elects to the White House, a candidate who misunderstands these basic facts, the likelihood of ever substantially addressing immigration is nil.

And the backward tactics of Alabama will likely spread to other states.

3

Offering In-State Tuition Rates to Illegal Immigrants Violates the Law

Hans A. von Spakovsky and Charles D. Stimson

Hans A. von Spakovsky was the counsel to the assistant attorney general for civil rights at the US Department of Justice from 2002 to 2005. Charles D. Stimson served as a federal prosecutor and later deputy assistant secretary of defense in 2006 and 2007. Both are currently senior legal fellows in the Center for Legal & Judicial Studies at The Heritage Foundation, a conservative public policy think tank.

The Illegal Immigration Reform and Immigrant Responsibility Act of 1996 prohibits state universities and colleges from offering illegal aliens in-state tuition rates on the basis of residence if the same is not done for all citizens of the nation (meaning, students who are born in the country but may not be from the state in which they attend college). Several states have flouted this law, creating exemptions that supposedly permit illegal aliens to acquire in-state tuition based on their completion of high school or attainment of a GED (high school equivalence diploma) in the state where they live. This course is deceptive and illegal, for it still grants a privilege to illegal aliens while denying it to other citizens. Since the majority of American taxpayers do not believe in subsidizing tuition for illegals, the federal government needs to enforce the law and put an end to this favoritism.

In 1996, Congress passed—and President Bill Clinton signed into law—the Illegal Immigration Reform and Immigrant Responsibility Act (IIRIRA). Section 1623 of this federal statute prohibits state colleges and universities from providing in-state tuition rates to illegal aliens "on the basis of residence within the State" unless the same in-state rates are offered to all citizens of the United States. Today, 12 states allow individuals who are in the United States illegally to pay the same in-state tuition rates as legal residents of the states—without providing the same rates to others. By circumventing the requirements of § 1623 these states are violating federal law, and the legal arguments offered to justify such actions are untenable, no matter what other policy arguments are offered in their defense.

A Nation of Laws, Not of Men

The United States is a country of immigrants—men and women who sought opportunity and freedom in an exceptional new land. Americans take pride in their heritage and this country's generous policies regarding legal immigration. Yet, as citizens of a sovereign nation, Americans retain the right to decide who can and cannot enter this country—and what terms immigrants and visitors must accept as a condition of residing in the United States. As mandated by the U.S. Constitution, Congress sets America's immigration policy. State officials have considerable influence in Congress over the crafting of immigration laws, and they may take steps to help enforce federal law. However, state officials cannot act contrary to a congressional statute.

America is a "nation of laws, not of men," and thus her citizens must abide by the rule of law. But even if the operation of the rule of law was not imbedded in the U.S. Constitution and legal system, every generation of Americans should re-affirm its virtue and security. These concepts, ancient as they are, and quaint as they may sound to some, provide the bedrock principles of this nation's constitutional republic. To abandon them in individual cases—where, for example, it seems opportunistic or personally appealing—is to render them unavailable in the preservation of all other rights.

It is obvious that Congress meant to prohibit state colleges and universities from offering in-state tuition to illegal aliens unless the state institutions also offer in-state tuition to all students.

The Constitution, the States, and Immigration

Article 1, Section 8, Clause 4 of the United States Constitution provides that Congress has the power to "establish an uniform Rule of Naturalization." Over the decades, Congress has done just that, imposing a variety of conditions on those who wish to immigrate (e.g., such individuals must do so openly and in accordance with established legal process) and on those who might be visiting (e.g., such individuals must not overstay their authorized visit).

Unambiguous federal law regarding who may receive the benefit of in-state college tuition is part of these conditions. Specifically, § 1623 of IIRIRA provides that

> Notwithstanding any other provision of law, an alien who is not lawfully present in the United States shall not be eligible on the basis of residence within a State (or a political subdivision) for any postsecondary education benefit unless a citizen or national of the United States is eligible for such a benefit (in no less an amount, duration, and scope) without regard to whether the citizen or national is such a resident.

Thus, it is obvious that Congress meant to prohibit state colleges and universities from offering in-state tuition to illegal aliens unless the state institutions also offer in-state tuition to all students, regardless of whether they live in the state or in another state. Congress may have assumed that state colleges and universities would not be able to "afford" offering in-state rates to everyone because these schools rely on the higher tuition from out-of-state students to help subsidize public colleges, and thus they would not offer in-state rates to illegal aliens. But the law itself provides a choice and only requires states to treat out-of-state citizens and illegal aliens equally.

Alternative criteria [that states use to provide illegal aliens with in-state tutition rates] are intended to act as a substitute for actual residence, which, in turn, creates the patina of compliance with the federal statute.

IIRIRA, once signed into law by President Clinton, should have settled this issue. But some states have continued to offer lower tuition to illegal aliens without offering the same to all students—a direct violation of federal law. Specifically, 12 states have circumvented the express language and clear intent of the statute by erecting proxy legal justifications for offering in-state tuition to illegal aliens. These states have asserted these legal arguments in courts and forced others to waste time and resources in litigation to try to enforce federal law. Such state policies not only violate federal law; they also:

- Encourage illegal immigration;

- Are fundamentally unfair to students from out of state who are U.S. citizens; and

- Force taxpayers to subsidize the education of illegal aliens.

Beyond these immediate concerns, there is another, larger issue at stake: the federal government's preeminent power to regulate immigration. The Supreme Court has held [in *De Canas v. Bica* (1976)] that the "[p]ower to regulate immigration is unquestionably exclusively a federal power." However, not every state action "which in any way deals with aliens is a regulation of immigration and thus *per se* pre-empted by this constitutional power, whether latent or exercised." In order for a state statute affecting immigrants (legal or illegal) to be valid, it cannot be expressly preempted by federal immigration law and must "not otherwise conflict with federal law" [as stated in *Chamber of Commerce v. Whiting* (2011)].

State laws that provide in-state tuition rates to illegal aliens are both expressly preempted by, and in conflict with, § 1623—unless the state also provides in-state tuition rates to all other American students regardless of their state of residence. However, none of the states that provide in-state tuition rates to illegal aliens have changed their state laws to provide such tuition rates to out-of-state students who are U.S. citizens.

Circumventing Federal Law 101

To avoid IIRIRA's mandate that in-state tuition be determined "on the basis of residence within a State," some state lawmakers have created alternative criteria through which students might qualify for in-state tuition. Such alternative criteria are intended to act as a substitute for actual residence, which, in turn, creates the patina of compliance with the federal statute: Since residence is not at issue, there is, so these states argue, no conflict between federal and state law. In reality, however, the states are targeting illegal aliens for in-state tuition.

Maryland's Senate Bill 167, which was signed into law by Governor Martin O'Malley (D), is a typical example of such chicanery. This bill exempts individuals, including "undocumented immigrants," from paying out-of-state tuition if the person attended a secondary school in the state for at least three years, graduated or received a GED [high school equivalence diploma] in the state, proves that he or his parents have filed Maryland income tax returns annually for the three years the student attended school in Maryland, and states that they will file an application to become a permanent resident.

Maryland Attorney General Douglas F. Gansler provided a dubious legal opinion regarding Senate Bill 167 to Gov. O'Malley on May 9, 2011. Gansler concluded that federal law (in particular, 8 U.S.C. § 1623(a)) does not preempt Senate Bill 167. The opinion suggests that Senate Bill 167 is not subject to the preemptive effect of § 1623(a) because the former "looks to factors such as time of attendance in Maryland schools and graduation from Maryland schools to define an exemption from nonresident tuition" and not residence. There are at least two problems with that legal analysis.

First, federal law permits a state to grant in-state college tuition to an illegal alien only if the state affords the same benefit to non-Maryland residents. The purpose of that law is to allow a state to treat illegal aliens like nonresidents for college tuition purposes: If the state does not charge more to the latter than to in-state students, then it may charge the same amount to illegal aliens (who, in an abstract sense, are akin to non-Marylanders). But Maryland's law does not use that formula; Gansler claims that the bill does not require "residence" in Maryland to attend college and receive in-state tuition since it looks to "time of attendance" in Maryland high schools.

However, the regulations of the Maryland Board of Education authorize local schools to require "proof of the residency of the child" for admission into public schools for kindergarten through high school. In fact, the Web site for the Prince George's County Public Schools says that "proof of residence shall be a prerequisite of admission to the public schools" and parents and guardians who are registering their children for school the first time must file an "Affidavit of Disclosure as required by law, *verifying their legal residence* in Maryland." Montgomery County also tells parents enrolling their children for the first time that "all students . . . must provide verification of age, identity, *residency*, and immunizations." As the state's attorney general, Gansler has constructive knowledge of this residency requirement. The fact that he ignores it throws into question the premise on which his entire legal opinion rests.

No one who lives in, and went to high school in, for example, Wyoming, could satisfy the eligibility requirements of Senate Bill 167; the new law does not apply to non-Marylanders. As such, because the Maryland bill does not put non-Maryland residents on a par with Marylanders, the bill cannot give illegal aliens a break on state tuition.

Second, Gansler's letter states that "the entire purpose of the bill is to design a law that will enable the State to continue to provide services to young undocumented aliens." The purpose of the bill, therefore, is to achieve the result that Congress outlawed in 8 U.S.C. § 1623(a)—granting in-state college tuition to illegal aliens without also granting that benefit to non-Maryland residents.

Illegal aliens who have sued states for denying admission to post-secondary institutions as a violation of their constitutional rights have had their lawsuits thrown out.

The Supreme Court has repeatedly struck down state legislation enacted to evade federal statutory or constitutional requirements. Indeed, the Court has rejected such legislation even when state lawmakers do not reference a suspect or disfavored classification:

> The states have no power, by taxation or otherwise, to retard, impede, burden, or in any manner control, the operations of the constitutional laws enacted by Congress to carry into execution the powers vested in the general government.

For example, in 2000, the Court struck down a Hawaiian statute that limited voting in certain elections to individual descendants of those who lived in Hawaii prior to 1778. The statute's eligibility requirements made no mention of race but were an obvious pretext for Polynesian heritage.

These state statutes that are intended to provide in-state tuition to illegal aliens are similar pretextual attempts to evade the federal immigration statute.

The Martinez Legal Fig Leaf

The few federal cases on this issue filed by citizen university students and their parents against such state laws have not reached the substantive merits of the preemption issue because the courts have held that individuals do not have standing to sue under this statutory federal provision.

For example, in *Day v. Bond*, the Tenth Circuit Court of Appeals dismissed the lawsuit brought by nonresident citizen university students and their parents against the state of Kansas. Section 1623 does not create a private right of action and the plaintiffs lacked standing to bring an equal protection claim. The court held that the injuries claimed by the plaintiffs failed to satisfy "the requisite standing criteria." These injuries included:

1. The denial of equal treatment caused by the Kansas law that made it impossible for nonresident U.S. citizens to obtain the same in-state benefits;

2. The increased tuition faced by the plaintiffs since the burden of subsidizing illegal alien beneficiaries is passed along to other students through tuition hikes;

3. The harm that results from competition for scarce tuition resources; and

4. The extra tuition paid by nonresident plaintiffs during the academic year over the in-state tuition paid by nonresident illegal aliens, as a consequence of the discriminatory law.

On the other hand, illegal aliens who have sued states for denying admission to post-secondary institutions as a violation of their constitutional rights have had their lawsuits thrown out on the merits. In *Equal Access Education v. Merten*, a Virginia federal district court held that, although illegal aliens had standing to bring suit, Virginia was under no obligation to allow illegal aliens to attend Virginia colleges and universities. Virginia's law was not preempted by federal law and did not violate due process: "It defies logic to conclude that . . . Congress left states powerless to deny admission to illegal aliens." The court concluded that the "persuasive inference to draw from § 1623 is that public post-secondary institutions need not admit illegal aliens at all, but if they do, these aliens cannot receive in-state tuition unless out-of-state United States citizens receive this benefit."

As the National Conference of State Legislatures notes in a report on in-state tuition for illegal aliens, in order to try and "maneuver around the [§ 1623] requirements, the eleven states that have enacted laws granting in-state tuition rates to undocumented students have tried to word the legislation so that it is contingent on high school attendance and graduation, and not based on residency within the state." But Texas bases its definition of residency for college admission on an individual (or his parent) establishing domicile in Texas not later than one year before the academic term in which the student is enrolled in college or graduating from a Texas high school who "maintained a residence" continuously for three years before graduation. Similarly, California bases residency on high school attendance in California for three or more years and graduation from a California high school.

The California Supreme Court bought into this legally questionable argument in *Martinez v. Regents of the University of California*. The court recognized that the question of federal preemption of California's residency law depended on whether the three-year high school attendance requirement is an "exemption based on residence within California." However, the court held that the requirement that a student attend a California high school for three years and graduate was not a residency requirement. It overturned the California Court of Appeals, which had come to the legally straightforward conclusion that the California law was intended to benefit illegal aliens living in the state and the "wording of the California statute . . . creates a *de facto* residence requirement." The court of appeals did not consider it relevant that the eligibility criteria did not correlate 100 percent with residency.

An August 2011 Rasmussen poll found that 81 percent of voters oppose providing in-state tuition rates to illegal aliens.

The California Supreme Court made the illogical claim that because § 1623 is not an "absolute ban" on illegal aliens receiving such tuition benefits, that section of federal law is not in accord with the expressed intention of Congress in its immigration legislation to "remove the incentive for illegal immigration provided by the availability of public benefits." The court also ignored the fact that the state had adopted the law specifically to benefit illegal aliens living in California and that the overwhelming majority of those who qualified for the benefit were only illegal aliens.

While this legally erroneous decision may be the law in California (at least for the time being), it is not the law anywhere else in the country. Although the U.S. Supreme Court denied a petition of certiorari [a request to a higher court to review the case of a lower court] filed by the plaintiffs, it is black letter law that such a denial has no precedential effect whatsoever; this issue has not yet been decided on the merits by any federal court.

And yet, offending states continue to ignore the clear language provided by a federal court in the *Merten* decision, and instead rely on the preferred outcome found in a state supreme court ruling—a shortsighted and legally specious approach to governing.

Unwise Public Policy

Giving illegal aliens a financial break at state colleges and universities is not only illegal; it is also immensely unpopular with American taxpayers. An August 2011 Rasmussen poll found that 81 percent of voters oppose providing in-state tuition rates to illegal aliens. Seventy-two (72) percent of voters believe parents should be required to prove their legal residency when registering their children for public school.

These results, however, should hardly come as a surprise: In 2005, it was estimated that the cost to taxpayers of providing in-state tuition in California was between $222.6 million and $289.3 million, while the cost to Texas taxpayers was between $80.2 million and $104.4 million.

Granting financial preference to illegal aliens also discriminates against otherwise qualified citizen students from outside the state. Furthermore, states that offer in-state tuition to illegal aliens act as a magnet for more illegal aliens to come to the state. Arguments to the contrary are unpersuasive, and not supported by the facts.

An Obligation to Enforce Federal Law

States that offer in-state tuition for illegal aliens are in violation of federal law. In doing so, these states are also acting against the will of the American people.

The applicable statute and the case law are clear: If there is no private right of action under § 1623, the U.S. Department of Justice must enforce this statutory provision against states that have violated federal law. Yet even as it sues states like Arizona and Alabama for trying to assist the enforcement of federal immigration law, the U.S. government refuses to sue states that are incontrovertibly and brazenly violating an un-ambiguous federal immigration law.

The President and the Attorney General have an obligation to enforce the provisions of the United States' comprehensive federal immigration regulations—including the federal law prohibiting state colleges and universities from providing in-state tuition rates to illegal aliens "on the basis of residence within the State."

4

Lawmakers Should Pass the DREAM Act

Marshall Fitz

Marshall Fitz is director of the immigration policy program at the Center for American Progress, an institution dedicated to educating Americans about public policy and to advocating progressive change. Formerly, Fitz served as the director of advocacy for the American Immigration Lawyers Association.

First proposed to Congress in 2001, the Development, Relief, and Education for Alien Minors (DREAM) Act offers young undocumented immigrants a path toward citizenship if they have lived in the country for five years and either complete two years of higher education or military service. The act would affect only those immigrants who arrived in the country as minors and therefore would have no impact on subsequent migration; instead, it would benefit the children who were brought to America without having a say in the matter. Helping these young immigrants reflects the nation's ideals of offering opportunity to those who seek a better life. Passing the act would also reduce the taxpayers' burden of providing more social services to these potential wage earners, and it would create more taxpayers to help cut the nation's deficit. Congress needs to face this issue and finally pass the DREAM Act.

The arguments mustered in opposition to the Development, Relief and Education for Alien Minors Act, or DREAM Act, have never been particularly persuasive. It's hard to make a straight-faced argument against providing kids who lack immigration status through no fault of their own an opportunity to go to college or serve the country through military service.

The nonpartisan Congressional Budget Office ... concluded that the DREAM Act would reduce the deficit by $2.2 billion over the next 10 years.

That's why dozens of House members spoke in favor of the bill, which passed when it came to the floor on December 8 [2010]. Only a few hardliners stood to oppose it. The extreme broadsides levied by those House conservatives have been echoed by senators seeking to block consideration of the bill. More than anything, these deceptive arguments clearly expose the moral callousness of the opponents.

It's important to expose the flaws and blatant misrepresentations in DREAM Act opponents' most common arguments against the bill. It should be clear that the Senate has no good reason not to pass it.

The DREAM Act Is Affordable

Myth: America can't afford the DREAM Act.

Fact: America can't afford not to pass the DREAM Act.

One of the most baseless excuses for opposing the bill is fiscal. Opponents of the bill have tried to throw a series of sensational and utterly unsupported cost figures into the debate, hoping something will stick. But the nonpartisan Congressional Budget Office, or CBO, did the analysis and concluded that the DREAM Act would reduce the deficit by $2.2 billion over the next 10 years.

DREAM-eligible youths would not be eligible for health care subsidies, including Medicaid, or other federal means-tested benefits like food stamps or Pell grants. More importantly, the alternative of removing the 700,000 eligible kids would cost taxpayers $16.2 billion over five years.

The far stronger argument is: "America can't afford not to pass the DREAM Act."

The Act Would Not Subvert the Rule of Law

Myth: The DREAM Act would reward illegal behavior.

Fact: This isn't amnesty. Eligible youth who had no say in the decision to come to the United States would have to work hard to earn permanent residence, and the earliest they could gain citizenship would be 13 years.

Opponents grasp for the moral high ground with this feeble contention. The dubious claim that providing a path to legal status somehow violates our commitment to the rule of law is standard fare for opponents of immigration reform. But this tired "anti-amnesty" argument lacks all resonance when applied to this population.

These kids were brought to the United States before they had a say in their life circumstances. Denying them hope and opportunity is punishment for an act beyond their control. Enabling them to work hard and earn the privilege of citizenship is hardly "rewarding" illegal behavior.

To be sure, this bill is not a solution to the problem of illegal immigration. But neither is it a magnet for more undocumented migration.

Moreover, the hypocrisy of some of the elected officials who would condemn these kids to marginalization is shameful. Sen. David Vitter (R-LA), who has confessed to moral waywardness, complains with a straight face that these kids are subverting the rule of law.

Affecting a Select Number of Immigrant Children

Myth: Passing the DREAM Act would encourage more illegal immigration.

Fact: The bill has strict requirements that make only a discrete one-time universe of individuals eligible for relief.

When immigration reform of any sort is under consideration the "magnet" excuse returns to vogue like clockwork. To be sure, this bill is not a solution to the problem of illegal immigration. But neither is it a magnet for more undocumented migration. And according to the secretary of homeland security the DREAM Act will enable DHS [Department of Homeland Security] to better focus its resources on criminals and security threats.

To be eligible for relief under the DREAM Act an individual must have come to the United States before they were 16 years old, and they must have been in the United States for more than five years on the date of enactment. In addition, they must be under 30 years old on the date of enactment and they must prove that they have possessed good moral character from the time they arrived in the United States. Those types of strict requirements—particularly the mandatory number of years in the United States—ensure there will be no surge of undocumented immigrants at the border.

No Chain Migration

Myth: The DREAM Act would trigger large-scale "chain migration."

Fact: It would be at least 10 years before a DREAM Act beneficiary could sponsor their spouse or child for permanent residence and at least 13 years before they could sponsor their parents or siblings.

Another claim rolled out with monotonous regularity is the "chain migration" excuse. Opponents falsely suggest that the nation's immigration system authorizes sponsorship of extended family, conjuring up hordes of great-aunts, step-uncles, and third cousins immigrating to the United States once the DREAM Act beneficiary gains legal status.

The reality is that our immigration laws only permit sponsorship of immediate relatives. And the soonest these youths would be able to sponsor their spouses or minor children to come to the United States would be 10 years after enactment. They could not sponsor their parents or siblings until after they became U.S. citizens, which is a minimum of 13 years after gaining legal status. Moreover, if their parents or siblings were in the United States unlawfully they would be required to leave the United States for 10 years before becoming eligible for sponsorship.

There are exponentially more boots and barriers on the ground at the southern border, and it is more secure than ever in our history.

A 23-year wait to bring your parents to the United States doesn't square with the chain migration menace promoted by opponents.

Border Security Is Already a Priority

Myth: We have to secure the border before doing anything else on immigration.

Fact: Our border is more secure than ever.

A prevalent tactic designed to delay taking a position on immigration issues is the "sequence" excuse. "We have to secure our borders first" has become the most common and perhaps least defensible talking point to prevent consideration of immigration-related legislation.

In fact, the singular focus of our immigration policies for the last nine years has been ramping up resources and implementing enforcement strategies. There are exponentially more boots and barriers on the ground at the southern border, and it is more secure than ever in our history. We spend more than $17 billion each year on our immigration enforcement agencies—a 70 percent increase over the last five years. And just six months ago we added another $600 million in emergency funding.

An Issue That Congress Has Time to Address

Myth: We can't bother with issues like the DREAM Act when we have more pressing priorities.

Fact: It is not an either/or proposition. Congress can address more than one important issue at a time.

During this lame duck period we've seen a new delay tactic deployed: the "prioritization" excuse. Yes, there is an array of pressing priorities facing the country right now requiring congressional attention. Sadly the one issue senators opposing the DREAM Act leveraged to try to block progress on the nation's agenda was way down that list: tax breaks for the wealthy. If they showed as much concern for the next generation as they do for millionaires they would realize that this is an investment in future leaders, thinkers, and entrepreneurs.

Dealing with the expiring tax cuts was certainly an important topic for congressional attention. But it should not have been to the exclusion of other critical issues. We elect our officials on the assumption, or at least the hope, that they can walk and chew gum at the same time. With the tax cut debate now in the rearview mirror, some senators are pivoting to argue that we are out of time and that impinging on the holidays is sacrilegious. What is truly immoral is that these senators would try to put their vacations before the lives of these youths.

No Time to Delay

Myth: We need more time to analyze the DREAM Act.

Fact: The basic elements of the bill are well understood and have been considered many times over the last nine years.

Last but not least is the process excuse, a standard ploy to justify delaying a vote. Opponents complain that numerous versions of the bill have been introduced and they need more time to thoroughly analyze it.

Preserving the status quo is to accept system failure and allow these youngsters to languish unproductively on the margins of society.

But this is not a new or complicated bill. The basic elements of the DREAM Act are straightforward, well understood, and have been considered numerous times over the last nine years. It has been introduced every Congress since 2001. It passed the Senate Judiciary Committee by a 16-3 vote in October 2003. And it passed the Senate Judiciary Committee again in 2006 by voice vote as part of the McCain-Kennedy comprehensive bill, which passed the full Senate by a 62-36 margin.

America Has Waited Long Enough

We have three basic options for addressing the situation confronting these young undocumented people: deport them to a country they barely know; preserve the status quo and consign these talented kids—who include valedictorians—to a hopeless future; or pass the DREAM Act and give them an opportunity to work hard and earn the privilege of citizenship.

The first and second options are morally bankrupt and fiscally irresponsible. As mentioned earlier, deporting the 700,000 youths whom the Congressional Budget Office has concluded would qualify for benefits under the bill would cost taxpayers about $16.2 billion over five years. Preserving the status quo is to accept system failure and allow these youngsters to languish unproductively on the margins of society. Both options run counter to Americas economic interests and to core American values.

The truth is, only the third alternative—passing the DREAM Act—makes economic, practical, and moral sense. Indeed, most (but not all) of the bill's opponents fear the politics around the bill more than they object to the substance. That tension between fear of the far right's backlash and what's right as a matter of policy and justice has driven them to evade the obligations of governance. The evidence of evasion lies in the transparent dissembling used to justify preventing a vote.

It's time for Congress to quit machinating and start solving problems. No more stale, flimsy excuses. The American public strongly supports the DREAM Act. The time has come for Congress to stand and deliver. This dream has waited long enough.

5

Lawmakers Should Reject the DREAM Act

Michelle Malkin

A syndicated columnist for Creators Syndicate, Michelle Malkin has maintained an online writing presence and contributed to the Fox News Network. She is also the author of four books, including Culture of Corruption: Obama and His Team of Tax Cheats, Crooks, and Cronies.

The Development, Relief, and Education for Alien Minors (DREAM) Act provides young undocumented immigrants a path toward citizenship if they have lived in the country for five years and either complete two years of higher education or military service. While seemingly a charitable act, the bill is really a means for the Democratic party to increase their electoral power among Hispanics. The ploy is transparent because federal law prohibits postsecondary benefits to illegal aliens unless comparable benefits are given to all US citizens. The DREAM Act has never passed Congress in a decade of attempts, and voters are not eager to support advantages for illegal immigrants over the many US-born students who struggle to attain higher education. For these reasons, lawmakers should continue to oppose this act.

The so-called DREAM Act [Development, Relief, and Education for Alien Minors Act] would create an official path to Democrat voter registration for an estimated 2 million, college-age illegal aliens. Look past the public relations-savvy stories of "undocumented" valedictorians left out in the cold. This is not about protecting "children." It's about preserving electoral power through cap-and-gown amnesty.

Deception That Should Not Fool Voters

Senate Majority Leader Harry Reid announced this week [in September 2010] that he's attaching the DREAM Act to the defense authorization bill. With ethnic activists breathing down his neck and President [Barack] Obama pushing to fulfill his campaign promise to Hispanics, Reid wants his queasy colleagues to vote on the legislation next week. Open-borders lawmakers have tried and failed to pass the DREAM ACT through regular channels for the last decade. That's because informed voters know giving green cards to illegal alien students undermines the rule of law, creates more illegal immigration incentives, and grants preferential treatment to illegal alien students over law-abiding native and naturalized American students struggling to get an education in tough economic times. This bad idea is compounded by a companion proposal to recruit more illegal aliens into the military with the lure of citizenship (a fraud-ridden and reckless practice countenanced under the [George W.] Bush administration).

DREAM Act lobbyists are spotlighting heart-wrenching stories of high-achieving teens brought to this country when they were toddlers. But instead of arguing for case-by-case dispensations, the protesters want blanket pardons. The broadly-drafted Senate bill would confer benefits on applicants up to age 35 and the House bill contains no age ceiling at all. The academic achievement requirements are minimal. Moreover, illegal aliens who didn't arrive in the country until they turned 15—after they laid down significant roots in their home country—would be eligible for DREAM Act benefits and eventual U.S. citizenship. And like past amnesty packages, the Democrat plan is devoid of any concrete eligibility and enforcement mechanisms to deter already-rampant immigration benefit fraud.

States Violating the Law

The DREAM Act sponsors have long fought to sabotage a clearly worded provision in the 1996 Illegal Immigration Reform and Immigrant Responsibility Act (IIRIRA) that states:

Americans across the political spectrum favor tougher enforcement of existing immigration laws over rolling out the amnesty welcome wagon.

"Notwithstanding any other provision of law, an alien who is not lawfully present in the United States shall not be eligible on the basis of residence within a State (or a political subdivision) for any postsecondary education benefit unless a citizen or national of the United States is eligible for such a benefit (in no less an amount, duration, and scope) without regard to whether the citizen or national is such a resident." Ten states defied that federal law and offered DREAM Act-style tuition preference lo illegal aliens: California, Illinois, Kansas, Nebraska, New Mexico, New York, Oklahoma, Texas, Utah, and Washington. The last time the DREAM Act champions tried to tack their scheme onto a larger immigration proposal, they snuck in language that would absolve those ten states of their law-breaking by repealing the 1996 law retroactively—and also offering the special path to green cards and citizenship for illegal alien students.

Despite the obvious electoral advantage this plan would give Democrats, several pro-illegal alien amnesty Republicans crossed the aisle to support the DREAM Act, including double-talking Sens. John McCain, Richard Lugar, Bob Bennett, Sam Brownback, Norm Coleman, Susan Collins, Larry Craig, Chuck Hagel, Kay Bailey Hutchison, Mel Martinez, Olympia Snowe, and presidential candidate Mike Huckabee (who champions even greater illegal alien student benefits than those proposed by Democrats). After paying lip service to securing the borders, McCain promised DREAM Act demonstrators this week that he supported the bill and would work to "resolve their issues."

Americans Support Tougher Immigration Laws

Out-of-touch pols might want to pay attention to the world outside their bubble. A recent Quinipiac University poll shows that Americans across the political spectrum favor tougher enforcement of existing immigration laws over rolling out the amnesty welcome wagon. When asked "Do you think immigration reform should primarily move in the direction of integrating illegal immigrants into American society or in the direction of stricter enforcement of laws against illegal immigration?", solid majorities of registered Republicans, Democrats and independents chose stricter enforcement over greater integration of the illegal alien population.

Democrats outside the Beltway have grown increasingly averse to signing on to illegal alien incentives—especially as the Obama jobs death toll mounts and economic confidence plummets. Here in Colorado, a handful of Democrats joined Republican lawyers to kill a state-level DREAM Act amid massive higher ed budget cuts and a bipartisan voter backlash. Asked why she opposed the illegal alien student bailout, one Democrat lawmaker said quite simply: "I listened to my constituents."

An alien concept in Washington, to be sure.

6

Educating Illegal Immigrant Children Yields Net Gain for the Country

Ronald Trowbridge

Ronald Trowbridge is a senior fellow at the Center for College Affordability and Productivity, a research center in Washington, DC, that examines, among other things, tuition rates and financial aid packages as they relate to student outcomes.

According to research, providing in-state tuition rates to children of illegal immigrants would result in an economic advantage for America because it creates more gainfully employed taxpayers. Continuing to bar these young people from achieving a college education simply yields more welfare recipients. Furthermore, if lawmakers insist that in-state tuition benefits subsidize immigrants unfairly in comparison to poor native-born children, then they need to examine the higher education system, which provides more financial subsidies to those attending wealthier colleges than to those that handle the bulk of the poor and middle class. The best option is to provide more support to the college enrollees that come from the social classes that can least afford tuition costs, and those include the children of undocumented immigrants.

Ronald Reagan once said, "Don't be afraid to see what you see." The current flap over [Texas] Gov. Rick Perry's defense of in-state tuition for students whose parents are in the United States illegally drives us to take off the lid and take a peek.

And what we see is that illegal-immigrant students pay back more than they take.

Daniel Griswold, an immigration expert at Cato Institute, wrote to me recently in response to my inquiry, "In 1997, the National Research Council [NRC] published a major study on immigration. It found that an immigrant with a college education is a huge net plus for the United States."

Griswold reports this finding of the NRC study: "Immigrants and their descendants represent a net fiscal gain for the United States. The typical immigrant and all of his or her descendants represent a positive $80,000 fiscal gain to the government. An immigrant with more than a high school education (plus descendants) represents a $198,000 fiscal gain, one with a high school diploma a $51,000 gain, and one with less than a high school education a $13,000 loss."

Looking at the Numbers

Some will counter that college slots for illegal immigrants should be given instead to poor U.S.-born students. But most of these students cannot afford college. Tuition, for example, at Texas' universities will average this year about $8,500, and the College Board projects that the average student's living expenses will be $17,820—for a total of $26,320. Multiplying this figure by five—now the Texas standard for number of years to graduation—totals $131,600.

But total costs will be higher than this. In Texas between 1999 and 2010, average tuition and related fees at the state's 10 largest universities rose by 120 percent. Tuition and fee increases of 10 percent a year will raise the figure of $131,600 to $160,591 in five years.

Let us look at immigrant subsidies, using Texas A&M University as a representative example. In-state tuition there is $8,418, out-of-state tuition $23,808—a yearly subsidy to illegal immigrants of $15,390. The total for five years is $76,950, plus a 10 percent annual increase in tuition—for a grand total subsidy of $93,957. Subtracting $93,957 from the $198,000 fiscal gain that the NRC study documented leaves a net gain of $104,043.

The dirty little secret that universities and state and federal legislators don't want the public to know is that these universities and legislators are de facto agents of class warfare.

Presently, the Texas Higher Education Coordinating Board reports that Texas colleges and universities currently enroll slightly more than 1.5 million students. Hispanic enrollment numbers are up this year by 4.5 percent—a very small increase in a state where 40 percent of all residents are Hispanic.

The number of illegal immigrants enrolled in public four-year colleges and universities in Texas totals 4,000, while the number in community colleges totals 12,000—still a very small percentage in a state that is 40 percent Hispanic. The in-state tuition subsidy in community colleges to illegal immigrants is about $2,000 a year. At Lone Star Community College, where I teach, in-state tuition is $1,744, out-of-state tuition $3,844.

Subsidizing Class Warfare

This is part of a larger problem and pattern. An October [2011] study by the American Enterprise Institute [AEI] entitled "Cheap for Whom?" finds: "Average taxpayers provide more in subsidies to elite public and private schools than to the less competitive schools where their own children are likely being educated."

The dirty little secret that universities and state and federal legislators don't want the public to know is that these universities and legislators are de facto agents of class warfare. Note the shocking disparity between the rich and the poor that AEI reports: "Among not-for-profit institutions, the amount of taxpayer subsidies hovers between $1,000 and $2,000 per student per year until we turn to the most selective institutions. . . . Among these already well-endowed institutions, the taxpayer subsidy jumps substantially to more than $13,000 per student per year."

It is class warfare. AEI argues, "If the country is to retain its competitive edge, it must reverse the current policies that result in providing the lowest levels of taxpayer support to the institutions that enroll the highest percentage of low-income, nontraditional, and minority students—the fastest-growing segments of the population."

And this should include illegal-immigrant students, who are residents of the state and pay sales and property taxes. They will pay back more than they take.

7

Children of Illegal Immigrants Cost Taxpayers Billions Each Year

Frosty Wooldridge

A vocal proponent of anti-immigration policy in America, Frosty Wooldridge has been a journalist for many years, writing editorials in newspapers such as the Denver Post *and the* Christian Science Monitor. *He is also the author of* America on the Brink: The Next Added 100 Million Americans *and other books.*

Many undocumented Mexican and other Latino immigrants come to America to take advantage of the welfare system by giving birth to "anchor babies," children that give them a permanent tie to the country and its social services. These children use up medical, educational, and even correctional resources—all at the expense of taxpayers. With political leaders unable or unwilling to stop this madness, it is unlikely that future Americans will survive the onslaught of illegal immigrants.

Average Americans fail to understand the enormous ramifications of 400,000 anchor babies born within the United States annually. They swamp our hospitals, ER wards and school systems. They cost taxpayers billions for "free" breakfasts and lunches along with English as a Second Language classes. Most of them flunk out of high schools, at which point, they either become pregnant themselves or join gangs. As they turn to the dark side, they fill our prison systems.

Unlawful immigrants and their children make up 29 percent of our local, state and federal prisons at a cost of $2.2 billion annually.

The mind-bending costs, according to Edwin Rubenstein, National Research Center, 2008 report, showed unlawful immigration costing American taxpayers $346 billion annually across 15 federal agencies.

In 1994, 74,987 anchor babies in maternity units cost taxpayers $215 million in Stockton, California.

Readers Respond to the Crisis

A reader said, "Great article about anchor babies becoming instant US citizens. I live in New York City . . . the amount of Mexicans having babies here is CRAZY! When I pick up my children at school I see Mexican mothers pregnant over and over, again and again, year after year. That's our city, state and federal government at work! But wait! The Chinese are number two after the Mexicans! It's unstoppable!"

Another reader said, "This event is easily prevented. The child's birth initiates this question to the mother: WHO HAS CUSTODY OF THIS CHILD? If the Mother answers that she has custody, then the Mother and child are sent to her home nation. If the Mother denies custody, the State takes custody of the child and sends the Mother to her home nation. The Citizen rights of the child are not invoked until age 21 years of age. Results: No anchor baby, no family attachment, no flood of future births in the US, problem solved. Our Government has flimflammed this nation into accepting these 3rd world immigrants to enhance thoughtless voters."

A third reader said, "Could it be that our congressmen refuse to address the anchor baby problem because they are afraid of mass race rioting and boycotts? The Latino population is quite possibly the most ethnocentric of all the ethnicities. Most of them want what they perceive is best for Latinos; regardless of the consequences for all ethnicities, and regardless of what is best for America. I am afraid that our politicians are afraid to feel their wrath, and to avoid bloodshed in the streets, and massive boycotts of products and services, they do nothing. Or, as I have stated before, maybe Americans simply admire Latinos, and are willing to sacrifice everything as long as they are assured Latinos will take over America."

The Costs of Anchor Babies

In 1994, 74,987 anchor babies in maternity units cost taxpayers $215 million in Stockton, California. In 2003, 70 percent of the 2,300 babies born in San Joaquin General maternity ward were from illegal aliens. That number has exploded today with over four million illegal aliens residing in California. Nine out of ten babies born in Parkland Hospital in Dallas, Texas stem from unlawful immigrant mothers. The figures for Chicago, New York City, Miami, Houston, Atlanta and other great cities run the same.

One lady, Linda Torres was arrested in Bakersfield with $8,500.00 in small bills in her pocket. It was her SSI lump award for her disability, which was heroin addiction.

The French economist Frederic Bastiat said, "The unseen is more expensive than the seen." In Stockton, California, the Silverio Family was featured in the *Wall Street Journal* in 2003. They were fruit pickers who arrived illegally from Oxtotilan, Mexico in 1997. The wife, Felipa had three kids, but popped an anchor baby named Flor. The child was premature and spent three months in a neonatal incubator at a cost to the San Joaquin Hospital of over $300,000.00. They conceived another, Christian. The second baby made them eligible for $1,000 per month welfare. Because Flor is disabled, she receives $600.00 monthly for asthma. Although the illegal aliens made $18,000.00 annually picking fruit, they collected $12,000.00 of your tax dollars for their anchor babies. One night the father, Cristobal crashed his van. He had no license or insurance. Taxpayers paid for all hospital bills. That's why 77 hospitals in Border States were going bankrupt in 2003, but Senator John McCain wrote a rider into the Medicaid Bill for $1.4 billion of your tax dollars. It passed.

Not to finish the spending spree on these anchor babies, the children attend California schools at a cost of $7,000.00 per year over and above what their parents pay in taxes. The cost for all five of their children for one school year exceeds $35,000.00 times 18 years for a grand taxpayer total of $630,000.00. This is only one family. No wonder California is $26 billion in debt.

Additional costs for illegal alien children stem from translators, advocates and middlemen. Medi-Cal in 2003 sponsored 760,000 illegal aliens. Supplemental Security Income is a non-means-treated federal grant of money and food stamps. Be assured that scams and fraud run rampant. Over 500,000 'mentally disabled kids' are on drugs for ADHD and ODD. One lady, Linda Torres was arrested in Bakersfield with $8,500.00 in small bills in her pocket. It was her SSI [Social Security Insurance] lump award for her disability, which was heroin addiction.

Just so Americans across the country don't feel left out, let's move to Georgia. Net Fiscal Costs of Illegal Immigration for Georgia:

Births of illegal aliens in Georgia cost to taxpayers:

2000—5,133 births cost: $13 million

2001—9,528 births cost: $23 million

2002—11,188 births cost: $27 million

Additionally, receiving public assistance in 2002 for 25,000 children of illegal aliens cost Georgia taxpayers $42 million annually. Health care costs to Georgia taxpayers for illegal aliens in 2002 featured 64,000 doctor visits which ran Grady Health System into a $63 million deficit.

Lawmakers Support This Fraud

What is it in your state? This picture is a small window into the massive fraud being perpetrated on your wallet by your congressional leaders. What is your senator or congressman doing about it? The simple answer fulfills French economist Bastiat's rule of the unseen. Your congressional reps assist this fraud! They encourage it every day by doing nothing about 2,200 illegal aliens crossing our borders and they have done nothing since 9/11 [2001] to deport the estimated 13 million that are already here.

With over three million illegal aliens arriving annually, they birth 300,000 anchor babies in California alone and you pay the maximum. When those legal 'American' babies grow to 18, they can 'chain migrate' their kin into our country. We're talking about a crisis SO huge, your children and this country will not survive it.

8

Children of Undocumented Immigrants Are Not US Citizens

Vincent Gioia

A retired patent attorney, Vincent Gioia is a contributing editor to Family Security Matters, an online forum for engaging American citizens on issues of national security.

Some Americans believe that the Fourteenth Amendment confers citizenship upon everyone born within the United States. This is a misguided interpretation of the amendment, and one that unfortunately has been supported in a misguided Supreme Court case. Legislative history and other court cases, however, clearly show that the Fourteenth Amendment grants citizenship only to those people who are born in the country and do not owe allegiance to another, foreign power. Undocumented immigrants are not American citizens because they have not officially renounced their ties to their home countries. Because they have not done so, their children are also still bound through national allegiance to their parents' homeland.

A common misconception is that the Constitution through the Fourteenth Amendment confers citizenship upon everyone born in the United States whether or not they were born to an illegal alien. Actually, the Constitution itself does not provide citizenship to those born of illegal parents; the

Supreme Court only said it did in an 1898 decision known as *U.S. v. Wong Kim Ark*, and it is politically correct to accept this Supreme Court decision while ignoring others.

Ignoring the Fourteenth Amendment

The problem is that the court majority in the Wong Kim Ark case, as is so often today, 'made law' according to their personal beliefs and not what those that wrote the Constitution (or in this case, the 14th Amendment) actually intended at the time it was written. Justice Horace Gray, who wrote the majority decision in the Wong Kim Ark case, reveals exactly what the majority was up to by avoiding discussion about the intention of the clause by the two Senators most responsible for the language of the Fourteenth Amendment, Senators Jacob M. Howard and Lyman Trumbull.

It is clear the court majority in this case recognized the only reasonable way to come to the conclusion they wanted was to ignore the recorded legislative history left behind by the writers of the amendment. Justice Gray acknowledged this when he wrote:

> "Doubtless, the intention of the congress which framed, and of the states which adopted, this amendment of the constitution, must be sought in the words of the amendment, and (sic)[but] the debates in congress are not admissible as evidence to control the meaning of those words."

Justice John Paul Stevens disagreed with this attempt by the Wong Kim Ark majority to rewrite the Constitution:

> "A refusal to consider reliable evidence of original intent in the Constitution is no more excusable than a judge's refusal to consider legislative intent."

Justice Gray and the court majority refused to consider both the original intent and legislative history behind the words because they knew it would be fatal to their predetermined intent of reversing what Congress had inserted into the US Constitution by the fourteenth amendment so they avoided what senators Howard and Trumbull wrote and said.

The Overlooked Intent of the Fourteenth Amendment

Why did Justice Gray avoid the legislative history and the original intent of those writing the 14th amendment?

Well the first major hurdle Senator Howard presented to the court majority in this case is that he specifically declared the clause to be by *"virtue of natural law"* and national law only recognized citizenship by birth to those who were not subject to some other foreign power. The Senator also stated when he introduced the amendment:

> "The clause [the citizenship clause section 1] specifically excludes all persons born in the United States who are foreigners, aliens, and persons who belong to the families of ambassadors or foreign ministers accredited to the Government of the United States, but will include every other class of persons."

It seems clear that the amendment only applies to American citizens (natural law), regardless of their race—which is exactly what was intended. Remember, the amendment was written after the Civil War with the intent to acknowledge the citizenship of those who had been slaves, not foreigners subject to national laws of other countries and not already citizens of the United States.

Illegal aliens and visitors do not enjoy the same quality of jurisdiction as a citizen of the United States.

The court majority had an even bigger problem to impose their will on American citizens because Senator Howard also said in May, 1868, that the

"Constitution as now amended, forever withholds the right of citizenship in the case of accidental birth of a child belonging to foreign parents within the limits of the country."

Senator Trumbull, the co-author, additionally presents a problem for the court majority by declaring:

"The provision is, that 'all persons born in the United States, and subject to the jurisdiction thereof, are citizens.' That means 'subject to the complete jurisdiction thereof.' What do we mean by 'complete jurisdiction thereof?' Not owing allegiance to anybody else. That is what it means."

Sen. Howard followed that up by stating that:

"The word 'jurisdiction,' as here employed, ought to be construed so as to imply a full and complete jurisdiction on the part of the United States, whether exercised by Congress, by the executive, or by the judicial department; that is to say, the same jurisdiction in extent and quality as applies to every citizen of the United States now."

Illegal Aliens and Their Children Owe Allegiances to Foreign States

Illegal aliens and visitors do not enjoy the same quality of jurisdiction as a citizen of the United States. Can an alien be tried for Treason against the United States? Senator Howard clearly intended that the phrase *"subject to the jurisdiction"* does not apply to anyone other than American citizens.

The writer, John A. Bingham, of the 14th amendment's first section, considered the proposed national law on citizenship as

"simply declaratory of what is written in the Constitution, that every human being born within the jurisdiction of the United States of parents not owing allegiance to any foreign sovereignty is, in the language of your Constitution itself, a natural born citizen. . ."

Ironically, the Supreme Court had already decided the meaning of the 14th amendment's citizenship clause before the Wong Kim Ark case, and unlike the majority in the Wong Kim Ark court, did consider the intent and meaning of the phrase "*subject to the jurisdiction*". In the Slaughterhouse cases [*Slaughterhouse Cases Butchers' Benevolent Association of New Orleans v. The Crescent City Livestock Landing and Slaughterhouse Co.* (1873)] the court noted that

> "[t]he phrase, 'subject to its jurisdiction' was intended to exclude from its operation children of ministers, consuls, and citizens or subjects of foreign States born within the United States."

America's own naturalization laws from the very beginning never recognized children born to aliens to be anything other than aliens if the parents had not declared their allegiance to the United States.

Even the dissenting minority in the Slaughterhouse cases affirmed that the citizenship clause was designed to ensure that all persons born within the United States were both citizens of the United States and the state in which they resided, provided they were not at the time subjects of any foreign power.

Another Supreme Court decision [*Elk v. Wilkins* (1884)] correctly determined that

> "subject to the jurisdiction" of the United States required "not merely subject in some respect or degree to the jurisdiction of the United States, but completely subject to their political jurisdiction, and owing them direct and immediate allegiance."

America's own naturalization laws from the very beginning never recognized children born to aliens to be anything other than aliens if the parents had not declared their allegiance to the United States—a sure sign that the framers intended children under national law followed the citizenship of their father until he had become naturalized.

Supporting the Language and History of the Fourteenth Amendment

Also of interest, Justice [Melville] Fuller, chief justice of the court in the Wong Kim Ark case, said,

> "The words 'subject to the jurisdiction thereof,' in the amendment, were used as synonymous with the words 'and not subject to any foreign power."

He was absolutely correct.

Considering both the legislative and language history behind the citizenship clause (14th Amendment, Section 1)—and the courts own stated objective in reaching the conclusion they did while also taking into account two prior Supreme Court holdings—leaves the Wong Kim Ark ruling completely worthless. The decisions in the Slaughterhouse and Elk cases are still the only controlling case law that is fully supported by the history and language behind the citizenship clause as found in the first section of the 14th amendment, and it should be so today.

9

Children of Undocumented Immigrants Should Be Deported

Chet Nagle

Chet Nagle served in the US Navy as a carrier pilot during the early years of the Cold War, and subsequently became a Central Intelligence Agency (CIA) agent working in the Middle East. He later founded The Journal of Defense & Diplomacy *and has since continued consulting and writing about the defense industry in his retirement.*

In the past, America maintained a rigid policy of deporting immigrants who enter the country illegally. Today, liberal politicians have fought such policies by claiming the Fourteenth Amendment protects children of illegal immigrants from deportation. The Fourteenth Amendment says no such thing, and some conservative politicians are taking appropriate steps to pass legislation that would emphasize the fact that children of illegal aliens are aliens themselves and worthy of deportation. So far, right thinking politicians have been thwarted in converting such legislation into law, but soon taxpayers will wake up to the financial burden of illegal immigration and reinstate stricter deportation measures.

In the 1930's, 1940's and 1950's the United States deported trainloads, busloads, and shiploads of illegal aliens. "Operation Wetback," ordered by President [Dwight] Eisenhower in

1954, charged the Immigration and Naturalization Service (INS) with deporting a million illegal aliens: men and women and their American-born minor children. Government agents did it then, and the 14th Amendment to the Constitution does not prevent them from doing it today.

Was the operation effective? In ninety days 750 INS agents, with state and local police, deported 80,000 illegals from Texas alone. Thousands more were deported from California, Arizona, Utah, Nevada and Idaho. And while the operation was underway, 488,000 illegals in Arizona and California returned to Mexico on their own; another 700,000 fled Texas.

Misapplying the Fourteenth Amendment

Liberal Democrats cling to the 14th Amendment and say deportation of American-born children to the homeland of their parents will never happen again. They point to the first sentence of Section 1: "All persons born or naturalized in the United States, and *subject to the jurisdiction thereof*, are citizens of the United States and of the State wherein they reside." (Emphasis added.)

Mexican illegal aliens are subject to the jurisdiction of Mexico, and so are all their children who are born here.

They also believe an 1898 Supreme Court case, *U.S. v. Wong Kim Ark*, governs the issue of birthright citizenship. In order to get the desired result, the court ignored the intentions of the framers of the 14th Amendment, and legislative history. Their decision stated, "the debates in Congress are not admissible as evidence to control the meaning of those words."

That was expedient, but wrong. How wrong? Senator [Jacob] Howard said, in May of 1868, that the "Constitution as now amended, forever withholds the right of citizenship in the case of accidental birth of a child belonging to foreign parents with the limits of the country."

An excellent study by Vincent Gioia, *Are Children Born of Illegal Immigrants US Citizens*, is in the "Family Security Matters" website for 15 July [2010]. The bottom line: Mexican illegal aliens are subject to the jurisdiction of Mexico, and so are all their children who are born here.

Politicians Ready to Act

When a study by the Federation for American Immigration Reform (FAIR) showed that illegal aliens cost U.S. taxpayers $113 billion per year, legislators began to think about their unemployed constituents. For example, Senator Lindsey Graham (R-SC) said that automatic "birthright citizenship" needs to be changed, and that he might introduce a constitutional amendment to that effect. Senate Minority Leader Mitch Mc-Connell (R-KY) and Senator Jon Kyl (R-AZ) agree in principle. They know, however, that Democrats would violently resist such an amendment in a Senate debate, and the required approval of 38 states would take forever.

> *The White House conspires with the Department of Homeland Security in order to legalize illegal aliens with a stroke of the president's pen.*

Former Representative Nathan Deal of Georgia had a better idea, and he introduced a bill proposing that being born in the U.S. only confers citizenship if one of the child's parents is a U.S. citizen. That bill has been kept in limbo by Speaker Nancy Pelosi for a year, even though at last count it has 92 sponsors. If passed, the law would undoubtedly be challenged by the great Americans of the ACLU [American Civil Liberties Union], lambasted by other great Americans in the mainstream media, and finally wind up before the Supreme Court. Today's justices would then be able to review the flawed decision in the Wong Kim Ark case and honor the intentions of the framers of the 14th Amendment. Better to do it now than later, when President [Barack] Obama might have an opportunity to appoint another Justice like Elena Kagan, and tip the court into left wing territory for decades.

Arizona State Senator Russell Pearce, a sponsor of the immigration law recently suspended by a liberal federal judge, is thinking about sponsoring an Arizona state law that also challenges the notion of birthright citizenship. If he is successful, such a new Arizona law would immediately attract high voltage lightning from the Obama administration and would go before the Supreme Court even faster than the bill proposed by Nathan Deal.

And as sensible congressmen gamely oppose an administration determined to grant amnesty to illegals, Arizona Sheriffs like "Sheriff Joe" Arpaio, Paul Babeu, Clarence Dupnik, and Larry Dever have million dollar bounties put on their heads by drug cartels. After one of his deputies was shot by drug-runners and tepid federal authorities continued to refuse to secure the border, Sheriff Babeu said, "Our own government has become our enemy."

A National Failure

While lawmakers ponder and lawmen patrol, the White House conspires with the Department of Homeland Security in order to legalize illegal aliens with a stroke of the president's pen. The plot has the Forest Service calling illegal aliens, "displaced foreign travelers!"

Our national failure to take a grip on reality is costing us dearly. In Texas the costs of illegal immigration, $16.4 billion, equals the state's entire current budget deficit. In California the cost is $21.8 billion, $8 billion *more* than the state deficit. And New York's deficit is only two-thirds of the $9.5 billion cost of that state's illegal population.

Who will be the first to stop paying for the children of illegal immigrants: unemployed workers, or ranchers in the vast borderland the cartels have seized from the United States?

10

The Government Must End the Child Tax Credit for Illegal Immigrants

David Vitter

Former member of the US House of Representatives, David Vitter now serves Louisiana in the US Senate. A Republican throughout his career, Vitter's platform has stood against amnesty for illegal immigrants as well as other more-liberal agendas, such as same-sex marriage and abortion rights.

Low-income working families in America are eligible for government checks to help cover the costs of raising children. However, illegal immigrants have learned that they can also apply for this tax credit and rake in undeserved taxpayer money. Currently, the country loses more than $4 billion a year to illegal immigrants through this credit loophole. This unjust reward must stop, and Congress needs to rally behind measures that would require applicants for the child tax credit to provide social security numbers in order to receive their checks.

Call it a loophole, tax fraud, or government at its most outrageous, but it's got to stop.

The federal government is currently handing out $4.2 billion in taxpayer-funded checks a year to illegal immigrants.

This isn't some service benefit that illegal immigrants are receiving like taxpayer-subsidized healthcare or education. And it's not a tax deduction or credit that requires the recipient to actually pay any taxes. It's a taxpayer-funded check from the federal government via the refundable Child Tax Credit program. And there's absolutely no proof required that the recipient actually be eligible under the law, which illegal immigrants are not.

Abuse of this tax benefit is one of the most ridiculous factors adding to our country's federal deficit today. Equally harmful, it is acting as a powerful incentive for more illegal immigrants to come to America—a magnet for more and more illegal crossings and activity.

Handing Out Checks to Illegal Immigrants

While it is true that illegal immigrants can't qualify for legitimate Social Security numbers and use them to file income tax returns, many illegal immigrants have discovered that the IRS [Internal Revenue Service] allows them to apply for Individual Taxpayer Identification Numbers (ITIN). And the overwhelming majority of returns filed using ITINs are filed by illegal immigrants—this is how they fraudulently apply for and receive these checks.

This tax credit was designed to help working families offset the costs of raising children. But the practical reality is that illegal immigrants—who don't possess valid Social Security numbers because they are not authorized to legally work in this country—are currently able to receive these tax credits by simply providing an ITIN and claiming children who might not even live in the United States. So, American taxpayers are writing checks to illegal immigrants—$1,000 per child, $4.2 billion per year total.

An investigative reporter in Indianapolis recently uncovered cases in which illegal immigrants were claiming the Child Tax Credit for nieces and nephews who did not even live in the United States. Some received more than $10,000 from the federal government.

One illegal immigrant interviewed in Indiana admitted that his address was being used by four other illegal immigrants who don't live there. They claimed 20 children were living in one mobile home and received tax returns totaling $29,608. But only one child was observed to actually live at the residence. The 19 other children live in Mexico and have never visited the United States.

Tragically, the IRS is doing nothing to police against this blatant fraud.

Fighting Government Inactivity on Such Costly Abuse

The [Barack] Obama administration's own Department of Treasury, through its Inspector General for Tax Administration, has repeatedly warned about these abuses and said that "millions of people are seeking this tax credit who, we believe, are not entitled to it."

Tragically, the IRS is doing nothing to police against this blatant fraud. While I believe it could and should, the agency's complete inaction has prompted me to introduce a clear solution in Congress—the Child Tax Credit Integrity Preservation Act—that would prevent illegal immigrants from claiming these tax credits intended for hard-working American citizens.

My bill is simple and workable. It would require every individual applying for the Child Tax Credit to provide a valid Social Security number, exactly as everyone must do to receive the earned income credit.

Sen. Jeff Sessions (R-Ala.) and I took to the Senate floor recently to ask our Senate colleagues to pass this common-sense bill by unanimous consent.

Unfortunately, none other than Senate majority leader, Harry Reid (D-Nev.), blocked our effort.

This reform is badly needed. We must act—particularly now, in tough economic times, when every American family is scrubbing its budget and demanding that Congress do the same. So I'll keep fighting until it's done.

The American people have the innate common sense and fairness to see this plain as day. The question is: will this U.S. Senate muster up those same qualities and do the right thing?

11

Children of Illegal Immigrants Struggle When Parents Are Deported

Marjorie Valbrun

Marjorie Valbrun is a staff writer for America's Wire, a news service of the Maynard Institute's Media Center on Structural Inequality. She writes about politics, immigration, and race, and her articles have appeared in the Wall Street Journal, The Washington Post, *and other major outlets.*

When undocumented immigrant parents are deported by US authorities, their children are often remanded to foster care. The system attempts to provide these children with needed care, but it often ignores the rights of the parents who have no wish to surrender their sons and daughters. Unfortunately, US immigration law often presumes the children are better off in US custody than with their parents because it deems a life in American foster care more beneficial than a life of poverty in many immigrant homelands. US lawmakers should rethink this assumption and see the value in reuniting families instead of tearing children from parents.

More than 5,000 children of immigrants are languishing in state foster care nationwide because their parents were living in the United States illegally and were detained or deported by federal immigration authorities.

These children can spend years in foster homes, and some are put up for adoption after termination of their parents' custody rights. With neither state nor federal officials addressing the problem, thousands more are poised to enter the child welfare system every year.

"They can be dropped into the foster care system for an indefinite period of time," says Wendy D. Cervantes, vice president for immigration and child rights policy at First Focus, a bipartisan advocacy organization in Washington, D.C. "This causes severe long-term consequences to a child's development. It has a negative impact on the country as a whole and a direct impact on taxpayers. The fact that these children have parents means they shouldn't be in the system in the first place."

Too often, these children lose the opportunity to ever see their parents again when a juvenile dependency court terminates parental rights.

Families Torn Apart

A recent report by the Applied Research Center (ARC), a national racial-justice think thank, found that when immigration enforcement methods intersect with the child welfare system, consequences for immigrant families can be devastating and long-lasting.

Jailed or deported parents are prevented from reuniting with their children, and parents held in immigration detention centers are penalized for being unable to attend hearings in family court. They are also penalized for not meeting court-ordered requirements for regaining custody of their children. The requirements are impossible to meet from jail.

In addition, detained parents often aren't aware that they can request that their children be returned upon deportation, placed with relatives in the United States, or allowed to return to their home countries. Parents unable to speak, read or write English, let alone understand complicated legal rulings, are often uninformed of their legal rights or where their children have been sent. They often don't have lawyers to help navigate the child welfare system.

"Immigration policies and laws are based on the assumption that families will, and should, be united, whether or not parents are deported," the ARC report states. "Similarly, child welfare policy aims to reunify families whenever possible. In practice, however, when mothers and fathers are detained and deported and their children are relegated to foster care, family separation can last for extended periods. Too often, these children lose the opportunity to ever see their parents again when a juvenile dependency court terminates parental rights."

Losing a Son to Adoption Services

Encarnación Bail, an undocumented immigrant from Guatemala, who is in a prolonged fight to regain custody of her son, has confronted many of these obstacles.

She lost custody of her infant son, Carlos, in 2008, a year and a half after she was arrested and jailed by federal immigration authorities during a raid of the poultry plant where she worked in Cassville, Missouri. Awaiting deportation, she spent two years in federal detention, first in a local county jail in Missouri and then in a federal prison in West Virginia. During her imprisonment, relatives caring for Carlos gave the baby to a local couple who were childless. After a county court terminated Bail's parental rights on grounds that she had abandoned the baby, the couple adopted her son.

The court sent an official letter to Bail informing her that the couple was caring for her son, but the letter never reached her and was returned unopened to the court. When a formal adoption petition did reach her, Bail was stunned. With the assistance of a prison guard and an English-speaking visitor from Guatemala, Bail wrote back that she did not want her son put up for adoption and wanted him placed in foster care until she was released. She also requested visitation with Carlos. She never received a response from the court and she was never informed about the custody hearings.

The government deported more than 46,000 parents of children with U.S. citizenship in the first half of 2011.

The Guatemalan government learned of her case through news reports and intervened on her behalf, prompting the American government to put the deportation order against her on hold and grant her temporary legal status allowing her to stay and work in the United States while she continues a legal battle to regain custody of Carlos.

"I'm very sad, I very much want to be reunited with him," Bail said through her lawyer. "I suffered an injustice. I'm the mother of Carlos and I was worried for Carlos during my entire detention. I was always thinking about him and I never gave my consent for his adoption."

Policy Versus Practice

The [Barack] Obama administration now says it is no longer targeting immigration enforcement activities on undocumented workers, such as Bail, and is instead focused on seeking out and deporting immigrants who have committed major crimes. However, immigrant advocates say that federal immigration agents, state law enforcement agencies and local county police departments participating in federal immigration enforcement programs do not follow that policy uniformly.

In fact, the government deported more than 46,000 parents of children with U.S. citizenship in the first half of 2011, according to the ARC report.

"It's clearly un-American to take kids away from loving families," says Rinku Sen, president and executive director of ARC. "It should give Americans real pause about what we're engaged in. We need to take a very hard look at these policies and practices." Hispanics make up the majority of undocumented immigrants in the United States and, as a result, children of color born to parents from poor countries in Latin and Central America and the Caribbean are affected disproportionally.

What's clear, say immigrant advocates, is that racial bias toward Latinos and other people of color play a significant role in separating children from parents and relatives.

Court transcripts strongly indicate that social workers' decisions about foster-care placements and judges' rulings on custody are sometimes driven by the feeling that the children are better off living in the United States with middle-class, white Americans rather than uneducated and unemployed parents who have been deported to poor home countries.

Furthermore, children in foster care are often not placed with relatives unless the relatives are here legally. Child-welfare workers consider undocumented relatives unsuitable foster parents because their status in the United States is unstable and they, too, can be detained or deported at any time.

Value Judgments Concerning Who Is a Suitable Parent

"There are definite judgments being made about the value of one particular family over another family," Sen says. Immigrants and their lawyers "have been told by officials in the child welfare and court system that a child placed in foster care is better off than being with family in Guatemala. There are racial biases that language and immigration status play into that we should be very careful about."

In Encarnación Bail's case, the judge who terminated her parental rights made clear in his ruling that he believed the adoptive parents, who make a comfortable living, were more suitable parents than Bail, whom he characterized as a serial lawbreaker. He wrote in his opinion that she, "would be unable to provide adequate food, clothing or shelter" to Carlos in the future.

[Current] laws give judges and child-welfare workers little latitude to reunify parents and children more easily.

"Encarnación is a human being, there's nothing quote unquote illegal about her," said Omar Riojas, who is her pro-bono attorney. "She lacked proper documentation to work; her defunct crime was one of immigration status, not of violence, not of larceny, not of any crime involving moral turpitude. Being undocumented does not render her unfit to be a parent."

Seth Freed Wessler, senior research associate at ARC and author of the report, says caseworkers told him that when parents are detained, "they fall off the face of the earth and when they are deported, it's even worse. It makes their job to reunify families all but impossible.

"Most caseworkers want that to happen but when immigration enforcement is involved, that outcome starts to rise. A whole set of systemic biases starts to emerge and take hold, a revealing assumption that children are better off in the United States no matter what, which ensures that children are not reunited with their families."

Planning Ahead in Case of Deportation

Marty Rosenbluth is executive director of the North Carolina Immigrant Rights Project, a nonprofit in Durham [North Carolina] that works to protect rights of people in deportation proceedings. He says laws give judges and child-welfare workers little latitude to reunify parents and children more easily.

"People will get picked up on some minor violation and end up being deported without any due process or hearing,"

Rosenbluth says. "We try to slow down the process enough so people can make some plans."

The biggest fear of parents in the immigrant community, he says, is that they're going to be deported and forced to abandon their children. "My clients talk about it all the time," Rosenbluth says. "They ask, 'If I get deported, what's going to happen to my kids?'" He says he tells them to grant power of attorney in advance to someone who can take custody of their children.

"But even that is risky," says Rosenbluth, an attorney. "Do you want to sign over custody of your children to someone you may not know simply because they are legal? A lot of Latino organizations are now telling undocumented immigrants with children to have an action plan and to have certain documents prepared and signed.

Responsible enforcement includes letting parents have due-process rights and ensure the well-being of their children.

"I've seen several different models of these action-plan packs. They include power of attorney and representation forms to have others sell their car or their property. I tell them to have someone who they can trust and who has some kind of legal status. They ask if they can sign over custody to their pastor or to their priest, but there's only so many children pastors can take."

New Legislation to Help Immigrant Parents

Cervantes says that since release of the ARC report, First Focus has been "in more intense conversations" with the Obama administration about adjusting current enforcement policies to ensure that nonviolent, non-negligent parents are not detained, and if they are, that they can make arrangements for the care of their children.

Her organization also lobbies for congressional passage of legislation that would establish "nationwide protocols to help keep children with their parents or caregivers while immigration proceedings are underway, and guidelines for certain immigration enforcement activities that involve parents, guardians, or primary caregivers of minor children."

"Responsible enforcement includes letting parents have due-process rights and ensure the well-being of their children," she said. The Humane Enforcement and Legal Protections for Separated Children Act, also known as the HELP-Act, was introduced in the Senate by Al Franken (D-Minn.), and Lynn Woolsey (D-Calif.) introduced a companion bill in the House. Both are stalled. Cervantes says the ARC report gives advocates momentum to make a new push for passage.

Meanwhile, Bail is now back in Missouri and working in a turkey processing plant. A year ago [in 2011], the Missouri Supreme Court unanimously overturned the judgment terminating her parental rights and the adoption of Carlos and ordered a new trial scheduled to begin on February 28 [2012]. She is optimistic that the court will rule in her favor.

"God is listening to my prayers," she said.

Organizations to Contact

The editors have compiled the following list of organizations concerned with the issues debated in this book. The descriptions are derived from materials provided by the organizations. All have publications or information available for interested readers. The list was compiled on the date of publication of the present volume; the information provided here may change. Be aware that many organizations take several weeks or longer to respond to inquiries, so allow as much time as possible.

American Civil Liberties Union (ACLU)
125 Broad St., 18th Floor, New York, NY   10004
(212) 549-2500
website: www.aclu.org

ACLU is the preeminent organization in the United States dedicated to protecting the civil rights and liberties of all Americans and individuals within the country. The organization's main areas of focus include First Amendment rights, equal protection under the law, due process, and privacy. With regard to immigrants, the ACLU seeks to ensure that even though immigrants may not be citizens, their rights as guaranteed by the Constitution and Bill of Rights are observed and protected. Accordingly, the organization takes special note of the rights of undocumented immigrants' children with a range of articles and publications exploring this issue available on the ACLU website.

**American Enterprise Institute for Public
Policy Research (AEI)**
1150 Seventeenth St. NW, Washington, DC
(202) 862-5800 • fax: (202) 862-7177
website: www.aei.org

AEI is a nonpartisan public policy organization that conducts research on pertinent policy issues, publishes its findings for the public and policymakers to review, and makes suggestions on future policy directions. The organization's research on immigration covers policy reform, skilled versus unskilled immigrants, and demographic research. Detailed policy reports and commentary on these issues and others can be found on the AEI website under the "Immigration" issue heading.

American Immigration Control Foundation (AIC Foundation)
222 W. Main St., PO Box 525, Monterey, VA   24465
(540) 468-2022 • fax: (540) 468-2024
e-mail: aicfndn@htcnet.org
website: www.aicfoundation.com

The AIC Foundation has sought since its founding in 1983 to inform Americans about the need for immigration reform. The organization believes that maintaining the current levels of immigration threaten American values and the livelihood of the country's citizens. Booklets published by the organization include titles such as *Assimilation: The Ideal and the Reality*, *Miami Today—The US Tomorrow*, and *The Path to National Suicide: An Essay on Immigration and Multiculturalism*, all of which can be downloaded from the foundation's website.

Americas Program
Cerrade de Xolalpa 7-3, Colonia Tortuga
   Mexico
011-52-555-324-1201
e-mail: info@cipamericas.org
website: www.cipamericas.org

As part of the Center for International Policy, the Americas Program works to improve development and cooperation in the Western Hemisphere by tackling the environmental, security, economic, and social problems that have traditionally stifled these goals. The program seeks to increase dialogue and understanding between the countries of the Americas by publishing policy reports, issue briefs, political commentary, and other educational materials. Articles on the organization's website, such as "The Modern Immigrant Rights Movement" and "Wall Street and the Criminalization of Immigrants," address issues related to the rights of undocumented immigrants' children.

Cato Institute

1000 Massachusetts Ave. NW, Washington, DC   20001-5403
(202) 842-0200 • fax: (202) 842-3490
website: www.cato.org

The Cato Institute is a public policy research organization dedicated to promoting the ideals of limited government, free markets, individual liberty, and peace in US government policy. The institute generally sees immigrants as contributing positively to the American culture, economy, and standard of living in the country, and sees their children as high-achievers in both school and society. Articles such as "Answering the Critics of Comprehensive Immigration Reform," "Immigration and the Welfare State," and "Is Birthright Citizenship Good for America?" address issues relating to the status of undocumented immigrants' children.

Center for Immigration Studies (CIS)

1522 K St. NW, Suite 820, Washington, DC   20005-1202
(202) 466-8185 • fax: (202) 466-8076
e-mail: center@cis.org
website: www.cis.org

CIS is an independent, nonpartisan think tank that seeks to increase the country's understanding of the economic, social, and demographic impacts of immigration in the United States. The organization espouses a low-immigrant stance based on the belief that limiting the number of immigrants allowed into the country will benefit both those who are granted citizenship and US citizens. Articles such as "Birthright Citizenship in the United States: A Global Comparison," "The Immigrant Paradox: The Stalled Progress of Recent Immigrants' Children," and "Illegal Alien Youths at Risk, Redux" cover topics affecting undocumented immigrants' children.

Council on Foreign Relations (CFR)
The Harold Pratt House, 58 E. 68th St., New York, NY   10065
(212) 434-9400 • fax: (212) 434-9800
website: www.cfr.org

As a nonpartisan, membership organization, CFR seeks to provide unbiased publications covering public policy issues currently impacting the United States. While the council is careful not to provide any official position statement within its reports, scholars working for the organization are able to present more argumentative commentary pieces and speak at conferences hosted by the organization. The CFR created a task force dedicated to assessing US immigration policy, and their findings were published in a report titled *US Immigration Policy*; additional articles discussing the issues related to the children of undocumented immigrants can be found on the CFR website.

Federation for American Immigration Reform (FAIR)
25 Massachusetts Ave. NW, Suite 330, Washington, DC   20001
(202) 387-3447
website: www.fairus.org

The FAIR membership organization calls for immigration reform that tightens border security to reduce the number of undocumented immigrants who enter the country and limits the number of legal immigrants allowed to enter the country—around 300,000 a year—to ensure US economic prosperity and security. Publications by the organization such as "Birthright Citizenship," "Paving the Road to Amnesty," and "Anchor Baby: Part of the Immigration-Related American Lexicon" provide detail and background to the concerns relating to the children of undocumented immigrants.

Heritage Foundation
214 Massachusetts Ave. NE, Washington, DC   20002-4999
(202) 546-4400 • fax: (202) 546-8328
e-mail: info@heritage.org
website: www.heritage.org

The Heritage Foundation is a conservative public policy organization that seeks to advance the ideals of free enterprise, competition, individual responsibility, limited government, and a strong national defense by promoting policies that embody these beliefs. The foundation supports states' rights to enforce immigration policies appropriate to maintain their citizens' rights, security, and livelihoods, and has called for comprehensive immigration reform to ensure this state level enforcement of immigration law is possible. Publications including "In-State College Tuition for Illegal Aliens and the Federal Law," "Defining Citizens: Congress Citizenship and the Meaning of the Fourteenth Amendment," and "Adding DREAM Act to Defense Bill Is Another Form of Amnesty" can be accessed on the Heritage website.

**National Network for Immigrant and
Refugee Rights (NNIRR)**
310 Eighth St., Suite 303, Oakland, CA   94607
(510) 465-1984 • fax: (510) 465-1885
e-mail: nnirrinfo@nnirr.org
website: www.nnirr.org

NNIRR has worked for more than twenty-five years to ensure that the rights of all immigrants and refugees, whether documented or undocumented, are observed and protected. Some of the organization's main areas of focus include fighting punitive immigration enforcement as implemented by local police forces and highlighting the human rights crisis on the US-Mexico border. Articles outlining the organization's campaigns and stances on these and other issues can be read online.

Pew Hispanic Center
1615 L St. NW, Suite 700, Washington, DC   20036
(202) 419-3600 • fax: (202) 419-3608
e-mail: info@pewhispanic.org
website: www.pewhispanic.org

Founded in 2001, the Pew Hispanic Center is a nonpartisan research organization that seeks to improve understanding of the US Hispanic population and to chronicle Latinos' growing impact on the nation. It is a project of the Pew Research Center, a nonpartisan "fact tank" in Washington, DC, that provides information on the issues, attitudes, and trends shaping America and the world. The Pew Hispanic Center conducts and commissions studies on a wide range of topics related to Hispanic life and culture in the United States, including the issue of immigration. It's website provides a number of articles, publications, statistical portraits, and surveys that deal with trends in both legal and illegal immigration in America, including matters concerning the children of undocumented immigrants.

Russell Sage Foundation (RSF)

112 E. 64th St., New York, NY   10065
(212) 750-6000
website: www.russellsage.org

The Russell Sage Foundation (RSF) has been working since its founding in 1907 to ensure the continual improvement of Americans' social and living conditions. For more than two decades RSF has assessed the impact of immigration on the country and researched the ways in which immigrants adjust to life in America. Publications such as "Assimilation's Bumpy Road" and *Immigrants Raising Citizens: Undocumented Parents and Their Young Children* explore the issues faced by undocumented immigrants and their children.

US Department of Homeland Security (DHS)

US Department of Homeland Security
245 Murray Lane SW, Washington, DC   20528
(202) 282-8000
website: www.dhs.gov

DHS is the government office charged with both ensuring the nation's security through the enacting of prevention and preparedness plans and overseeing immigration services and the US Customs and Border Protection, the law enforcement agency that patrols and physically secures the US border. Immigration statistics, enforcement, and the steps to becoming a citizen can be found on the DHS website.

Bibliography

Books

Irene Bloemraad — *Becoming a Citizen: Incorporating Immigrants and Refugees in the United States and Canada.* Berkeley: University of California Press, 2006.

Leo R. Chavez — *The Latino Threat: Constructing Immigrants, Citizens, and the Nation.* Stanford, CA: Stanford University Press, 2008.

Joanna Dreby — *Divided by Borders: Mexican Migrants and Their Children.* Berkeley: University of California Press, 2010.

David A. Gerber — *American Immigration: A Very Short Introduction.* New York: Oxford University Press, 2011.

Brooke Hauser — *The New Kids: Big Dreams and Brave Journeys at a High School for Immigrant Teens.* New York: Free Press, 2011.

Nancy S. Landale, Susan McHale, and Alan Booth — *Growing Up Hispanic: Health and Development of Children of Immigrants.* Washington, DC: Urban Institute, 2010.

Suzanne Oboler — *Latinos and Citizenship: The Dilemma of Belonging.* New York: Palgrave Macmillan, 2006.

Michael A. Olivas   *No Undocumented Child Left Behind*: Plyler v. Doe *and the Education of Undocumented Schoolchildren*. New York: New York University Press, 2012.

William Perez   *Americans By Heart: Undocumented Latino Students and the Promise of Higher Education.* New York: Teachers College Press, 2012.

William Perez   *We Are Americans: Undocumented Students Pursuing the American Dream.* Sterling, VA: Stylus 2009.

Alejandra Rincón   *Undocumented Immigrants and Higher Education: Sí Se Puede!* El Paso, TX: LFB Scholarly, 2010.

Yale Strom   *Quilted Landscape: Conversations with Young Immigrants.* New York: Simon & Schuster, 1996.

Carola Suárez-Orozco, Marcelo M. Suárez-Orozco, and Irina Todorova   *Learning a New Land: Immigrant Students in American Society.* Cambridge, MA: Belknap, 2008.

Daniel J. Tichenor   *Dividing Lines: The Politics of Immigration Control in America.* Princeton, NJ: Princeton University Press, 2002.

Hirokazu Yoshikawa — *Immigrants Raising Citizens: Undocumented Parents and Their Young Children*. New York: Russell Sage Foundation, 2012.

Periodicals and Internet Sources

Todd Beamon — "Just Dreaming?" *Diverse: Issues in Higher Education*, April 26, 2012.

Kevin Clarke — "Born in the U.S.A.," *U.S. Catholic*, October 2010. www.uscatholic.org.

Daysi Díaz-Strong et al. — "Dreams Deferred and Dreams Denied," *Academe*, May/April 2010.

Karin Fischer — "On Immigration Fault Line, Arizona Colleges Struggle for Balance," *Chronicle of Higher Education*, July 30, 2010. http://chronicle.com.

Daniel Glick — "Young, All-American, Illegal," *High Country News*, August 16, 2010.

C. Elizabeth Hall — "Where Are My Children . . . and My Rights? Parental Rights Termination as a Consequence of Deportation," *Duke Law Journal*, March 2011.

Lawrence Hardy — "The Costs of Immigration," *American School Board Journal*, April 2012.

Ingrid Hernandez — "Things I'll Never Say: Stories of Growing Up Undocumented in the United States," *Harvard Educational Review*, Fall 2011.

Laura A. Hernandez	"Anchor Babies: Something Less Than Equal Under the Equal Protection Clause," *Southern California Review of Law and Social Justice*, July 1, 2010.
Edith W. King	"The Plight of Illegal Immigrant Children in US Schools," *Race Equality Teaching*, Autumn 2010.
Julia Love	"Undocumented 'Dreamers' in College Welcome Policy Change on Immigration," *Chronicle of Higher Education*, July 6, 2012. http://chronicle.com.
Lesli A. Maxwell	"Immigration Law Casts Shadow over Schooling in Alabama," *Education Week*, June 7, 2012.
Laura Meckler, Miriam Jordan, and Andrew Seidman	"U.S. to Stop Deporting Some Illegal Immigrants," *Wall Street Journal*, June 16, 2012.
Russell Pearce	"Ending Birthright Citizenship," *Human Events*, June 28, 2010.
Eduardo Moisés Peñalver	"Birth Rights," *Commonweal*, September 24, 2010.
Felicia Persuad	"'Anchor Babies' Are Just Under 10 Percent of U.S. Births—So Quit Blaming Them," *New York Amsterdam News*, February 10, 2011. www.amster damnews.com.

Alejandro Portes and Alejandro Rivas

"The Adaptation of Migrant Children," *Future of Children*, Spring 2011. www.princeton.edu/futureofchildren.

Carola Suárez-Orozco et al.

"Growing Up in the Shadows: The Developmental Implications of Unauthorized Status," *Harvard Educational Review*, Fall 2011.

Robin Templeton

"Baby Baiting," *Nation*, August 16, 2010.

Peggy J. Hirschry Williams

"Victimizing the Victims: The Effects of US Immigration Laws on the Children of Illegal Immigrants," *Children's Legal Rights Journal*, Summer 2011.

Index